Reaching Gen Z with the Gospel in the College Classroom

Reaching Gen Z with the Gospel in the College Classroom

Awakening the Imago Dei in Gen Z

GREGORY J. RUMMO

Foreword by Nathan C. Lane

WIPF & STOCK · Eugene, Oregon

REACHING GEN Z WITH THE GOSPEL IN THE COLLEGE CLASSROOM
Awakening the Imago Dei in Gen Z

Copyright © 2025 Gregory J. Rummo. All rights reserved. Except for brief quotations in critical publications or reviews, no part of this book may be reproduced in any manner without prior written permission from the publisher. Write: Permissions, Wipf and Stock Publishers, 199 W. 8th Ave., Suite 3, Eugene, OR 97401.

Wipf & Stock
An Imprint of Wipf and Stock Publishers
199 W. 8th Ave., Suite 3
Eugene, OR 97401

www.wipfandstock.com

PAPERBACK ISBN: 979-8-3852-3334-2
HARDCOVER ISBN: 979-8-3852-3335-9
EBOOK ISBN: 979-8-3852-3336-6

01/31/25

Unless otherwise indicated, all Scripture quotations are from The ESV® Bible (The Holy Bible, English Standard Version®), © 2001 by Crossway, a publishing ministry of Good News Publishers. Used by permission. All rights reserved.

Scripture quotations marked (NIV) are from the Holy Bible, New International Version®, NIV®. Copyright © 1973, 1978, 1984, 2011 by Biblica, Inc.™ Used by permission of Zondervan. All rights reserved worldwide. www.zondervan.com.

Scripture quotations marked (NKJV) are from the New King James Version®. Copyright © 1982 by Thomas Nelson. Used by permission. All rights reserved.

Scripture quotations taken from the American Standard Version (ASV) and the King James Version (KJV) are in the public domain.

This project is dedicated to every student that has had the opportunity to be in one of my classes. I hope I was able to expand your understanding of the *imago Dei*[1] in your life through the gospel and how God is truly present in everything if we look for him. When we seek him, we will find him. There is no distinction between what is secular and what is spiritual. In many cases you have been the teacher and I, the student.

---

1. The *imago Dei* is Latin for the image of God. There is a rich and varied interpretation of this phrase by different theologians, including Irenaeus, Augustine, Aquinas, Luther, and Calvin, to name several. See Simango, "Imago Dei," 172–90. I have used this phrase throughout this project in the context of Palm Beach Atlantic University's statement of Kingdom Approach to Culture, Sexuality, Sanctity of Life, and Compassion: "We believe that all people are made in the imago Dei—the image of God (Genesis 1:26–27). This reality gives every human being intrinsic value and also compels us to treat each person with dignity, respect, kindness, understanding, love, and an eagerness to see them know God and fulfill their God-given purposes. . . . The imago Dei also undergirds our view of ethics and morality. That we are made in the image of God makes us eager to obey God and to live our lives according to His commands." Palm Beach, "Values and Guiding Principles," under "Worship, Workship, and Wordship."

Contents

List of Tables and Graphs | ix

Foreword by Nathan C. Lane | xi

Acknowledgments | xv

Preface | xvii

Introduction: Current Cultural Context at Palm Beach Atlantic University | 1

Chapter One: Having a Theological Vision | 14

Chapter Two: Know Their Stories | 22

Chapter Three: Developing an Ethos of "Extravagant" and "Intentional" Hospitality | 33

Chapter Four: Integrating Faith in the Chemistry Classroom | 47

Chapter Five: Integrating Faith in the Chemistry Laboratory | 76

Chapter Six: "Keller's Kids" | 88

Chapter Seven: Modeling Evangelism for Gen Z through Missions | 103

Chapter Eight: Conclusion and Success Metrics | 119

Bibliography | 127

Index | 137

List of Tables and Graphs

Table 1: Fall–Spring 2022–2023, Fall 2023–2024 (Three Semesters) Faith Journey Survey | 6

Table 2: University Statistics for Faculty Fall 2021–2022 | 9

Table 3: Number of Students Sharing Common Essay Themes 2020–2023 | 26

Table 4: Faith Integration Essay Topics for Pre-Nursing Cohort | 58

Table 5: Selected Seventies Soft-Rock Songs | 72

Table 6: Selected X Topics Posted | 73

Table 7: List of Materials Used in "Keller's Kids" | 99

Graph 1: CLG Attendance, February–November 2023 | 100

Foreword

SOME DISAGREEMENTS TAKE A long time to settle. In the academic world, few disputes have created deeper fissures than the relationship between faith and learning. Many wonder if a space where this feud might be settled even exists. Various institutions have pursued different options for resolution. One path that many schools have taken is the creation of two distinct spheres: learning and 'objective knowledge' occur in the classrooms and laboratories, while faith and 'subjective pursuits' are reserved for chapel and devotions. This bifurcated two-sphere approach, however, rarely yields good fruit and usually results in a deeply diminished role of 'faith' in the academy. Another option that schools have chosen is a model that openly embraces a Christian worldview as the lens through which knowledge is pursued. This second model seeks to bridge the objectivity demanded by the enlightenment and subjectivity of our faith convictions. A third, more recent approach among evangelical institutions, but with deeper roots in the Catholic faith, emphasizes not only the pursuit of knowledge but also the practice of our faith. This third approach seeks to engage students' heads, hearts, and hands.[1] Nevertheless, the fissure remains unbridged with many wondering if true unity is attainable.

---

1. For a fuller discussion of these three options, see Stephen Moroney, "Where Faith and Learning Intersect: Re-Mapping the Contemporary Terrain," *Christian Scholars Review* 43 (2014): 139–155.

FOREWORD

This work answers that question with a resounding, "YES"! Dr. Gregory Rummo's *Reaching Gen Z with the Gospel in the College Classroom* shows a successful pathway toward the intimate relation between faith and learning. *Reaching Gen Z with the Gospel in the College Classroom* provides substantial, granular examples of how one professor allows his faith to enliven his work among students. The model put forth by Rummo offers an expansive overview of how a faculty member can let their faith seep into every crevice of their work and details practical faith integration in the lecture hall, lab, Bible study, and co-curricular trips. For example, Chapter Four, "Integrating Faith in the Chemistry Classroom," presents an exploration into what a faith-infused chemistry classroom might look like—from pre-class discussions of pop culture to finding God in the subject matter content. The chapter also provides examples of how to help chemistry students, who are often headed into the medical professions to faithfully navigate stress, anxiety, and self-doubt. These concrete examples are the strength of the volume.

Dr. Rummo's lifetime of experience has given him the foundation to write such a book. Greg is a true Renaissance man! Having graduate degrees in chemistry, business, and theology, he has the qualifications to teach and excel in over half of Palm Beach Atlantic University's (PBA) schools. In addition to being a scientist and holding several patents, he served as CEO of a pharmaceutical company before his current faculty appointment at PBA. He has written hundreds of newspaper columns and actively consults in business and other disciplines. As an avid cyclist and family man who is fluent in multiple languages, it is clear that his life is one enlivened by his faith in Christ. Dr. Rummo is one of our students' favorite professors and they learn valuable lessons from him both inside and outside the classroom. Chemistry is not easy, but he makes it enjoyable and meaningful.

Reaching Gen Z with the Gospel in the College Classroom is an important work that bridges the faith and learning divide by providing tangible and applicable examples. At the most basic level, a clear argument for joining faith and learning would be useful but even better would be to give examples of how joining the two might be executed. Well, Rummo's work does just that. *Reaching Gen Z with the Gospel in the College Classroom* surpasses mere arguments and hypothetical examples by sharing a clear report of successfully bridging the gap. While the particulars of institutions differ, I am confident that this work will help inspire others as they seek to integrate faith and learning in their own contexts.

Nathan C. Lane

Acknowledgments

Can anyone be the artisan who fashions himself? Or is there any other spring from which being and living flow into us besides your making us Lord?

—Augustine[2]

GOD WASTES NOTHING IN the lives of his children. Almost every experience in my life has produced a fruit of competency, ordained by our sovereign Lord, and utilized in the crafting of this project. I came into this world from God, through my parents whom I did not choose. I was born in a place that I also did not choose. Since my beginning, I have depended on the people whom God placed in my life. I thank my parents who did their best to raise me in an environment of morality. I thank Nick Romano, a Yonkers, New York, fire fighter, who led me to Christ when I was nineteen years old. He has since gone on to his eternal reward. There have been over a dozen pastors whom the Lord has placed in my life. They, along with a longer list of full-time missionaries, other church leaders, close friends, and close, professorial colleagues at Palm Beach Atlantic University, and more recently, my professors at Knox Theological Seminary, have helped shape much of who I am today, especially my program and project advisor, Rev. Dr. Orrey

---

2. Augustine, *Confessions*, 1.6.10.

McFarland. But at the top of this list is Jenny, my wife of thirty-seven years, a graduate of Tennessee Temple University with a degree in missions. She has been the virtuous woman about whom Solomon wrote in Proverbs 31. She, along with our four children, James and John, our sons of thunder, and Rebecca and Rachel, our two adopted Chinese daughters, are precious gifts from God of inestimable worth. Whether aware of it or not, they have taught me much while giving me countless opportunities to have taught them a thing or two as their dad, teacher, and mentor.

—*Soli Deo gloria*

Preface

THE MAJORITY OF STUDENTS on college campuses currently are members of Generation Z (Gen Z). They are adults, born between 1997 and 2012, and the most stressed cohort to ever embark on their journey through higher education. They are reporting "the highest stress level" of any generation in the country, according to The American Psychological Association's (APA) "Stress in America 2020" report,[1] as well as the highest suicide rate. This is the field, white unto harvest (John 4:35), into which God has called professors at Christ-first institutions of higher education for such a time as this (Esth 4:14). The COVID-19 pandemic, which began in early March 2020, and sent all high school and college students home into virtual learning environments for the following eighteen months, exacerbated levels of stress, leaving some with feelings of hopelessness and depression. One recent study reported one in five Gen Zers have had thoughts of suicide.[2] This paper details my research into how best to reach Gen Z for Christ along with my ministry at Palm Beach Atlantic University, the place where the Lord has called me and given me the opportunity to

---

1. American, "Stress in America 2020," 3.

2 University of Queensland, "One in Five Adolescents." "Data collected from more than 275,000 adolescents aged between 12–17 years across 82 low, middle and high income countries . . . found 14 percent of adolescents had suicidal thoughts and 9 percent had anxiety over a 12-month period. The overall pooled prevalence was approximately one in five," paras. 2–3.

come alongside my students and help them recognize God's plan for their lives, utilizing methods and means anyone can institute to effectively reach students in higher education with the gospel. For a person contemplating a career in Christian higher education or for the professor already at a Christian university looking for ideas on how to reach his students for Christ, I put forth these suggestions as a model for ministering to Gen Z students at a Christian university.

Introduction
Current Cultural Context at Palm Beach Atlantic University

For God has not given us a spirit of fear, but of power and of love and of a sound mind.

—2 Tim 1:7 (NKJV)

INTRODUCTION

THE PURPOSE OF THIS project is to consider how best to reach Gen Z for Christ and to propose three methods for doing so. In this chapter I present my current cultural context at Palm Beach Atlantic University, along with the university's guiding principles for students and faculty, so that readers may understand the working location from which I am writing this project. I discuss the characteristics of Gen Z, and include for perspective a first-person, multigenerational narrative that demonstrates every generation has faced an existential threat. Also presented are the results with analysis of a three-semester survey of my students to assess their spiritual temperature. Finally, I discuss the university's three programs of worship, wordship, and workship that together provide a foundation to enlighten minds, enrich souls, and extend hands.

THE DREAM OF PALM BEACH ATLANTIC UNIVERSITY

Palm Beach Atlantic University began as a dream over fifty-five years ago in the mind of Dr. Jess Moody, the former pastor of First Baptist Church of West Palm Beach, currently Family Church Downtown.

> Founded under the providence of God with the conviction that there is a need for a university in this community that will expand the minds, develop the moral character and enrich the spiritual lives of all the people who may come within the orbit of its influence, Palm Beach Atlantic University shall stand as a witness for Jesus Christ, expressed directly through its administration, faculty, staff, and students.[1]

The Christ-first environment on campus—its current context if you will—is evangelical in theology and practice. Notwithstanding, the university is committed to offer "a curriculum of studies and a program of student activities dedicated to the development of moral character, the enrichment of spiritual lives and the perpetuation of growth in Christian ideals."[2]

STUDENTS

We practice a broad-minded embrace of students that come from diverse Christian denominations. In fact, sometimes it is very diverse. Several years ago, one of my students boasted that he was a proud atheist like his father. I stayed with him compassionately and prayed that the Holy Spirit would convict him. He eventually repented and believed in Jesus.

During the spring 2021 semester, I hired one of my former students to be one of my teaching assistants. She is Jewish. Students that decide to come here must be willing to fulfill chapel

---

1. Palm Beach, "Guiding Principles," para. 2.
2. Palm Beach, "Guiding Principles," para. 1.

INTRODUCTION

requirements. They come under the preaching of the word of God twelve times every semester.

Although a majority of the students here identify as Christian, many coming from evangelical denominations with a population of missionary kids and preacher's kids involved in local churches and having a heart for world missions, there are those who are not serious in their faith journey or, sadly, have no faith journey. These students in particular need to be pointed to Christ through the gospel. Adding to the urgency of the moment is that almost all of my students are members of Gen Z (ages 18–23). They are facing "unprecedented uncertainty, are experiencing elevated stress and are already reporting symptoms of depression."[3]

According to research published by Feed, a OneHope initiative, Gen Z is the most diverse generation ever.[4] Half are non-Caucasian. They are the least religious generation (51 percent in the United States say they are Christian but this has steadily declined over the last five years), giving rise to the phrase "The Nones"—those that have "none of the above" religious affiliation—which Barna reported comprised 34 percent in 2016.[5] Gen Z considers itself to be a "generation of authentic digital natives"[6] that is constantly connected. They are ambitious and possess an entrepreneurial spirit.

I can't help but wonder if at least part of the struggle of Gen Z with anxiety is the result of their parents having lived through 9/11, school shootings, the financial crisis of 2008, and wanting to protect their children from similar situations. The expression "helicopter parents" is borne from overprotective parenting. An anxious home environment affects the children and much of what they learn early on about life is caught as well as taught.[7]

Our parents and our grandparents (Gen Z's great-grandparents) faced existential crises in their lives and they didn't go

3. American, "Stress in America 2020," 1.
4. Feed, "What We Know About Gen Z."
5. Barna and Impact 360, *Gen Z*.
6. Feed, "What We Know About Gen Z."
7. Phillips, "Emotional and Social Health."

all to pieces. I often remind my students that what is needed is a multigenerational perspective on the COVID-19 pandemic and its lasting effects.[8]

Every generation has had some idealistic experience taken away from them by the harsh realities of living in an imperfect world marred by sin and distorted from the perfection that its Creator had in mind at the outset. My grandparents immigrated from Italy in the late nineteenth century when William McKinley was president. Like most immigrants, they came to America for a better life. It didn't get off to a great start. McKinley was assassinated six months into his second term in 1901. Thirteen years later the First World War began, lasting until 1918. Immediately following, the Spanish influenza pandemic infected five hundred million people worldwide, killing 10 percent of infected patients—3–5 percent of the world's population.[9] My grandparents also lived through the Great Depression, an economic crisis of unprecedented proportion, sparked by the 1929 stock-market crash. Tough times persisted for a decade. My grandfather lost his job. They almost lost their home.

One of their four children was my dad. He was born in 1920, thus a member of the Greatest Generation. He too lived through the Great Depression and later, as an adult, the Japanese attack on Pearl Harbor and the subsequent Second World War. My generation is the Baby Boomers. I grew up under the threat of nuclear annihilation at the hands of the Soviet Union and Cuba's Fidel Castro. The Cuban Missile Crisis in 1962 brought us to the brink of nuclear war.[10] As a kindergartner, I remember the drills in our public school. A warning siren sounded followed by the announcement, "Take safest places. Take safest places," and we went scurrying to our metal lockers away from the windows. Later in life, as a college freshman, the Vietnam War was winding down. Five years later, Reagan's presidency brought a calm to the world as the Berlin Wall crumbled and words such as *glasnost* and *perestroika* gave us hope that we would avoid mutually-assured destruction.

8. Rummo, "Multi-Generational Perspective."
9. All, "1918 Influenza."
10. Office, "Cuban Missile Crisis."

INTRODUCTION

Our two millennial sons were born into a time of relative calm until September 11 shattered our sense of security. We were living in New Jersey at the time, only eleven miles from the city. We could see the smoke rising from the rubble of the Twin Towers across the Hudson River. Then there was the anthrax scare shortly thereafter, a succession of wars in the Middle East, and the beheadings of innocent Americans by Islamic extremists. In 2003, we traveled to China to adopt our first daughter at the same time the world was learning about SARS. By the time we got back to the States, panic was ensuing in China, the truth finally making its way past the communist media censors. The same crowded places that we had visited as tourists only four weeks earlier were now deserted. Years later, when our sons graduated from college, they were faced with a bleak job market as the Great Recession took the economy down in 2010. We went back to China in 2005 to adopt another daughter; they are now both teenagers and members of Gen Z. They along with most of my students have grown up in a world marred by gun violence. Their "Take safest places," drills have been replaced by lockdowns. The truth is that we do not live in a garden of Eden. Each generation has faced its own challenges, some of them real existential threats. As I look back through four generations I can connect the dots, so to speak, and see God's hand. This is what I want for my students. University life post-COVID has resumed a calmer rhythm. The lesson here for them is that although we cannot see the future, there is no need to worry. "God gave us a spirit not of fear but of power and love and self-control" (2 Tim 1:7).

SURVEYING THE SPIRITUAL TEMPERATURE OF MY STUDENTS

Each semester I teach two cohorts of chemistry students. The majority are freshmen. The first and larger cohort is composed almost entirely of females studying nursing. The smaller cohort is composed of students concentrating on a variety of disciplines in the sciences: pre-med, pre-vet, various biology tracks, oceanography, zoology, environmental science, and forensic science. From the fall 2022 to the fall 2023 academic year, I conducted a survey[11] over these three semesters of 168 of my students. I wanted to assess their faith journey. I asked them their denomination, if they currently attended a church and if they were serving in that church, if they read their Bible and prayed regularly, if they believed they were led to Palm Beach Atlantic University, and if they had an interest in participating in a short-term mission trip. The following table shows the results of the survey based on the 127 respondents.

Table 1 Fall–Spring 2022–2023, Fall 2023–2024 (Three Semesters) Faith Journey Survey

DENOMINATION	RESPONSES
Evangelical	17
Baptist	28
Presbyterian	7
Roman Catholic	18
Lutheran	1
Jewish	1
Agnostic	3
Atheist	1
Non-Denominational	42
FAITH LIFE	
Read Bible and pray regularly	43
Read Bible and pray when I have time	52
I don't have a regular Bible and prayer life	27
I would like guidance in this area of my spiritual life	28

11. "As permitted by federal law and regulations governing the use of human subjects in research projects (45 CFR 46), the Palm Beach Atlantic University IRB has reviewed your proposed project titled Faith, Calling, and Mission Trips. The IRB has determined that the project qualifies as a Category II study (Expedited Review) approved under provisions established as part of IRB approval. Your research is approved to proceed." Dr. David Compton, Office of Academic Research at PBA, to author, Dec. 5, 2023.

CHURCH LIFE	
I currently attend a local church	98
I am serving in a ministry at a local church	32
I was active in my church at home	58
I am looking for a church	13
I don't care about church	4
CALLING AND MISSIONS	
I believe God led me to PBA	94
I have been on a mission trip	42
I would like to go on a mission trip	63

As table 1 shows, the majority of my students read their Bibles and pray (75 percent), attend a local church (77 percent), and believe God led them to PBA (74 percent). Many have been on a mission trip (33 percent), some multiple times, and about the same number would like to go on a mission trip or on another mission trip (50 percent). These findings are encouraging and, frankly, what one would expect at a Christian university.

Although I am passionate about all of my students, I am most concerned for those who indicated they are agnostics, atheists, don't have a regular devotional time (21 percent), would like some guidance in this area (22 percent), or are looking for a church (10 percent). These are the prodigals (Luke 15: 11–32) and the lost sheep (Luke 15:4–7), those whose rescue resulted in much rejoicing.

I make it a point to know each student's story[12] through a variety of methods that I will detail in chapter 3. I think it is important to know as many of my students personally as I can and it helps to be at a smaller Christian university. I assign papers for extra credit in which, as part of the prompt, I ask them to write about themselves, their family, where they are from, their faith journey, and why they came to Palm Beach Atlantic University. During scheduled meetings when a student comes to my office for tutoring, homework help, or to review an exam, I make it a point

12. Rummo, "Listen to Their Stories."

to chat with them about personal matters, especially if they have shared these in one of their assigned essays for my class. I almost always offer to pray with them before they leave. And if I am in my office and a student drops by unannounced for whatever reason, I engage them in informal conversation. This may seem like what one should expect of a professor at a Christian university but that is not always the case. Many professors have strict office hours and only see their students on those days and at those times. As I will argue in chapter 3, I think they are missing out on a potentially key strategy in connecting with Gen Z. Thus, all of my course syllabi list my official office hours followed by the statement: "If my lights are on and my door is open, feel free to drop in."

FACULTY

Many of my professorial colleagues attend evangelical churches, including our president, campus pastor, provost, and associate provost. This establishes a particular culture for the university. Everything rises and falls on leadership. The following chart provides a breakdown by gender and ethnicity of the current full-time faculty members as of the fall 2022 semester.

Table 2 University Statistics for Faculty Fall 2021–2022

RACE/ETHNICITY	MEN	WOMEN	TOTAL MEN + WOMEN
Non-Resident Alien	3	5	8
Hispanic/Latino	10	7	17
American Indian or Alaska Native	0	0	0
Asian	0	2	2
Black or African American	4	9	13
Native Hawaiian or other Pacific Islander	0	0	0
White	68	47	115
Mixed Races	0	1	1
Unknown	1	1	2
TOTAL	86	72	158

The university does not keep statistics regarding the religious denominations of its faculty; however, each member of the PBA community—faculty and staff—must agree to, teach in accordance with, and sign the university's guiding principles, which include belief in the inspiration of Scripture and the fundamentals of historic, orthodox Christianity (e.g., virgin birth, substitutionary atonement, resurrection).[13]

The ministry to which God has called me is manifold: to point my students to Christ, to disciple them, to mentor them, and to be in loco parentis as our associate provost encourages us. It is a balancing act between listening and speaking, empathy and advising, compassion and tough love, what they feel and what the Bible says.[14]

13. Palm Beach, "Guiding Principles."

14. Chapell, *Christ-Centered Preaching*, 93. "Our own relationship with Christ teaches us that we must treat people with compassion as well as confront them with the authority of the Word ... the soul made sensitive by the recognition of its own sin, the awareness of God's sovereignty, and the miracle of the Savior's love is the one best suited to guide the tongue in the sanctuary as well as in the circumstances of life."

WORSHIP, WORDSHIP AND WORKSHIP

Most if not all Christian universities have programs aimed at developing Christian character, conduct, and conversation. Palm Beach Atlantic University has adopted Worship, Wordship, and Workship. This catchy trio of nouns emphasizes the importance of honoring God with regular devotional times of prayer and Bible reading including attendance at chapel, the use of respectful, God-honoring speech with each other at all times, and service to the community, whether locally or on short-term international mission trips.

Palm Beach Atlantic University describes its culture as "Christ first." The university's statement of community values adds additional light, emphasizing that humans are made in the *imago Dei*—the image of God (Gen 1:26–27). This reality ascribes to every person "intrinsic value," compelling us to treat each person as we would want to be treated—with "dignity, respect, kindness, understanding, love, and an eagerness to see them know God and fulfill their God-given purposes."[15]

The university's motto is "enlightening minds, enriching souls, and extending hands." In the following section I will describe how this motto becomes a mission as it is lived out through three practices: Worship—honoring God in our character, conduct, and conversation; Workship—the university's community service program that provides opportunities for students to respond "to human needs with Christ-like action in the community and the world";[16] and Wordship—our conversation and how we use our words wisely, in a way that honors each other and Christ. The *imago Dei* also is the biblical basis for the school's views of ethics and morality. "That we are made in the image of God makes us eager to obey God and to live our lives according to His commands."[17]

---

15. Palm Beach, "Values and Guiding Principles," under "Worship, Workship, and Wordship." Additional statements on diversity, human sexuality, and the sanctity of life may be read on the same page.

16. Palm Beach, "Values and Guiding Principles," under "Worship, Workship, and Wordship."

17. Palm Beach, "Values and Guiding Principles," under "Worship, Workship, and Wordship."

Worship

Worship is encouraged in a number of venues, both informally and formally. Residence halls have discipleship leaders (DLs) that apply for this position through the Department of Ministry. They are interviewed and selected based on their desire to serve the Lord as spiritual peer mentors. They receive a scholarship for this position. Each DL then selects a number of volunteer discipleship assistants (DAs) and together they hold regular Bible studies, times of prayer, and informal worship in the residence hall to which they have been assigned.

I interviewed Rachel Hill, a nursing student and an MK (missionary kid), who served with her parents in Lusaka, Zambia, before moving to south Florida to attend Palm Beach Atlantic University. In addition to being a former student of mine, she also worked for me as a teaching assistant in one of the laboratory classes I teach. Her goal, along with the four DAs that she chose, is to "reach every student in [their] residence hall for Christ's sake."[18]

I mentioned worship earlier in this chapter with specific regard to chapel requirements for all students (faculty are *encouraged* to attend chapel). The university treats chapel as a course and "all full-time undergrad students are required to attend PBA Chapel at least 12 times during the fall semester and 12 times in the spring for a total of 24 chapel attendances for the Academic Year."[19]

In addition to the five-times-weekly chapel services offered in the university's DeSantis Chapel,[20] there are other opportunities throughout the year to earn chapel credits, among them attendance at Family Church's "PBA Day," held in late September; attendance at "Christival," a once-a-year series of special meetings when the university invites well-known speakers along with a popular, contemporary Christian band; and during mission emphasis week, when there are opportunities during evenings as well as regular chapel times.

---

18. Interview with Rachel Hill, Oct. 4, 2022.

19. Palm Beach, "Chapel," para. 1.

20. Chapel currently meets three times weekly in Family Church Downtown's seven-hundred-seat sanctuary.

Wordship

PBA's president, Dr. Debra Schwinn, came up with the idea for "wordship" as a description of using our everyday conversations as a means to worship and glorify the Lord. She tasked professor of communication and media ecology, Dr. Stephanie Bennett, to direct the program. Dr. Bennett is the author of *Silence, Civility, and Sanity: Hope for Humanity in a Digital Age*. The university offered a course in wordship during the spring 2022 semester titled Civil Discourse and the Common Good.

Dr. Bennett explains that wordship "is an act of worship, a way, that is, to help bring PBA students, staff, and faculty to a greater awareness and practice of using our words well and wisely. Learning how to be curious and non-judgmental about our differences is key. What is central to understanding Wordship is, we are all made in the image of God."[21]

Workship

Workship is the university's program that combines work and worship. It is a "distinctive community service program that responds to human needs with Christ-like action in the community and the world."[22] Students are required to complete forty-five hours of workship service per academic year. Recent efforts have included tutoring students at Conniston Middle School and Belvedere Elementary School, hurricane relief efforts in Puerto Rico, involvement with Urban Youth Impact, volunteering with the Palm Beach Children's Hospital Foundation, and packaging fifty thousand meals for hungry children. Over the past five decades, students have volunteered over 3.8 million workship hours.

---

21. Dr. Stephanie Bennett, email to author, Oct. 5, 2022. Printed with permission.

22. Palm Beach, "Workship."

INTRODUCTION

SUMMARY

As I have shown in this chapter, the cultural context at Palm Beach Atlantic University provides an excellent foundation upon which I can build a ministry specifically geared towards my Gen Z student cohort. In the pages that follow I will detail how I go about implementing the three components of my ministry based on the university's triperspectival call to enlighten the minds, enrich the souls, and help students extend their hands through specific examples of faith integration in my science courses, biblical hospitality in my school office, and missional opportunities in the developing world.

CHAPTER ONE

Having a Theological Vision

But seek the welfare of the city where I have sent you into exile, and pray to the Lord on its behalf, for in its welfare you will find your welfare.

—JER 29:7

INTRODUCTION

IN CHAPTER 1, I outlined the current cultural context at Palm Beach Atlantic University and the biblical foundation it provides for ministering to my Gen Z students. In this chapter I will build upon this foundation and describe my theological vision for effectively reaching them with the gospel. But first we have to answer the questions, What is a Christian university? What does it mean to be credentialed in servanthood? How important is mentoring? I will explore the answers of Dr. Kenneth G. Elzinga, the Robert C. Taylor Professor of Economics at the University of Virginia, in conjunction with the thoughts of the late Dr. Timothy Keller (1950–2023) from his book *Center Church*, in which he offers a template for effectively reaching people with the gospel through doctrinal foundation, theological vision, and ministry expression. By considering a university as a cultural center, we will apply Keller's template and develop an effective paradigm for reaching students with the gospel.

THE UNIVERSITY AS A CITY WITH A CULTURAL CENTER

A city can be thought of as a multicultural, multiethnic concentration of people living and working near one another, focused on their livelihoods. This sounds a lot like most universities. The population is diverse. Students live and work near one another. There is a commonality of purpose. Most schools have a governing code of conduct or a set of guiding principles to which all students must agree when beginning their four years of undergraduate study.

Of course, a university is not exactly like a city. The student population is not typically multigenerational, although the governing authorities and the faculty, a minority of the population nonetheless, help round this statistic out. Students that attend a university know it is a temporary way station in life. And a university by definition is a *uni*versity with a cultural center.

A Christian university, then, may be thought of as a cultural center with a unity of truth,[1] and that truth is the gospel. The gospel must be the guiding force shaping the culture at a Christian university, and the culture-shapers are the faculty, called to seek its welfare (Jer 29:7). They are the ones who spend the most time with the students and therefore have the largest potential for modeling Christian character in loco parentis. Shaping Christian culture at a Christian university is not a job to be left to "the Dean of the Chapel ... or the job of the Dean of Students' office."[2]

---

1. Litfin, *Conceiving the Christian College*, 79. "It has long been noted that the idea of a university as opposed to a multiversity, presupposes a unity of truth best safeguarded in the glad confession that all truth is God's truth."

2. Elzinga, "Christian Higher Education," 17.

THE THREE DISTINGUISHING CHARACTERISTICS OF A CHRISTIAN UNIVERSITY

Kenneth G. Elzinga cites three distinguishing characteristics of a Christian University.[3] The first is teaching. The classroom, the lecture hall, the laboratory all become places where Christian faith is supposed to be naturally integrated as part of the curriculum.[4]

Joel Carpenter, Calvin College's former provost, explains that the classroom at a Christian university is the place where a professor can "focus on questions of faith and knowledge and a Christian worldview. Every professor must in some sense become a lay theologian."[5] This sentiment is echoed by Graeme Goldsworthy, former lecturer at Moore Theological College and author of *According to Plan*, who writes, "All Christians are theologians, but some are more able theologians than others."[6]

Professors at Christian universities must be willing to assume the role of theologian, regardless of the academic discipline stated on their diplomas. Additionally, they are to look upon their role as missionaries, sent to the cultural center as if it were a city, where Scripture commands that they "seek its welfare" (Jer 29:7). Elzinga says that professors willing to assume this charge can play a significant role in helping to change the life of the students who are enrolled in their classes.

The second distinguishing characteristic of a Christian university is credentials, and not necessarily *academic* credentials. As Elzinga notes, "We put them before our names, after our names; we calibrate and quantify performance; we rank people all the

---

3. Elzinga, "Christian Higher Education," 14.

4. Elzinga, "Christian Higher Education," 14. "If the faculty members in Christian higher education simply believe their job is to teach what they learned in graduate school and then go home and be good church members, integration won't take place. And the school will produce a generation of students of which many will come to believe that there is a gap (if not a chasm) between the secular and the sacred."

5. As quoted in Dockery and Gushee, *Future of Christian Higher Education*, 117–18.

6. Goldsworthy, *According to Plan*, 29.

HAVING A THEOLOGICAL VISION

time; we look up to and look down on people according to performance-based credentials or titles."[7] However, "De-emphasizing [academic] credentials is a mark of Christian higher education."[8] We have only to look at the apostle Paul and how he, despite being one of the most learned theologians of his day, introduced himself as a privileged servant:[9] "Paul, a servant of Jesus Christ" (Rom 1:1); "Paul and Timothy, servants of Christ Jesus" (Phil 1:1).[10]

The third distinguishing characteristic of a Christian university is mentoring students in the same way that Christ mentored the disciples. Mentoring involves modeling for the students what it means to live the Christian life. This is also the role of the faculty, who hopefully have been pilgrims, sojourning through the world longer than the students, and have acquired wisdom through empirical data, so to speak, from sin, its consequences, and the resulting redemption.[11] Elzinga reminds us that Jesus invited his followers to become his disciples. Jesus is our ultimate example as professors in Christian institutions of higher education:

> Christian higher education exists because there once was a Galilean who made disciples. His disciples called Him rabbi, or teacher. And therein lies a principle by which teachers today are to invite—not coerce, but invite—students to be their disciples, that is, to mentor them. Jesus taught His followers the Law and the Prophets. But He

---

7. Elzinga, "Christian Higher Education," 15.

8. Elzinga, "Christian Higher Education," 15.

9. Harris, *Slave of Christ*, 127. Paul introduces himself as a *doulos*, "with the loss of the etymological sense of 'slave', 'bondsman' or 'servant' [with] the emergence of a new theological meaning, that of instrumentality (rather than servitude), of being Yahweh's chosen instrument (as in the case of Moses, Joshua or David) or tool (as in the case of Nebuchadnezzar or Cyrus) for the achievement of his purposes among humankind." *Doulos* here is not in the sense of unconditional subjection and bondage but "an official title of honor that stresses instrumentality and is reserved for a few men who are entrusted by God with special tasks in and for the church."

10. As a member of our university's servant leadership committee, I have emphasized to our hiring committee the importance of a candidate's testimony and not just his or her degrees, awards, and publications during interviews.

11. Elzinga, "Christian Higher Education," 17.

also lived among them and even washed their feet. I have often wondered what the Lord's illustration of foot washing means to the professoriate of the 21st century. Students in Christian higher education need to know that the faculty value the character and moral compass of their students: that professors admire godliness; that the faculty's deepest satisfaction as professors comes from seeing students become what God wants them to be—people for whom Jesus Christ is preeminent.[12]

How then can a professor at a Christian college allow Christ to animate these three characteristics to effectively reach Gen Z with the gospel? How can teaching in the classroom become discipleship, servanthood trump academic credentials, and mentoring become foot washing?[13]

The late Timothy Keller, pastor of Redeemer Presbyterian Church in New York City, developed a strategy of gospel renewal[14] to reach the church's cultural center. In his book *Center Church*, he explained that Redeemer's successes could be measured in terms of fruitfulness through a theological vision of a "restatement of the gospel with rich implications for life, ministry and mission in a type of culture at a moment in history."[15] I believe a similar model could be applied to my cultural center to reach students.

James Eglinton, the Meldrum Senior Lecturer in Reformed Theology at the University of Edinburgh, summarized the biblical basis for Keller's successful ministry in New York City:

> Keller spelled out how the doctrinal foundation of a church gives rise to a particular theological vision, which is a set of intuitions, sensibilities that guide how a church exists in its cultural surrounds. And that theological

---

12. Elzinga, "Christian Higher Education," 16.

13. At the beginning of every academic year, PBA has a foot-washing ceremony in the Rubin Arena. Leaders and student leaders wash the feet of all incoming freshmen.

14. Keller, *Center Church*, 54. "Gospel renewal is a life-changing recovery of the gospel. Personal gospel renewal means the gospel doctrines of sin and grace are actually experienced not just known intellectually."

15. Keller, *Center Church*, 20.

HAVING A THEOLOGICAL VISION

vision is then something that takes us to a third thing, which is expression of ministry. So, these three things are really important . . . doctrinal foundation, theological vision, ministry expression.[16]

We assume professors at Christian universities are doctrinally sound in their beliefs or they shouldn't be there in the first place.[17] But orthodoxy must become orthopraxy. Keller compares orthodoxy—or doctrinal foundation—to the hardware on a computer and orthopraxy—or ministry expression—to the software. Bridging belief and practice is "middleware," which he defines as theological vision.[18]

Richard Lints, professor of theology at Gordon-Conwell Theological Seminary underscores the importance of having a theological vision:

> A theological vision allows [people] to see their culture in a way different than they had ever been able to see it before. . . . Those who are empowered by the theological vision do not simply stand against the mainstream impulses of the culture but take the initiative both to understand and speak to that culture from the framework of the Scriptures. . . . The modern theological vision must seek to bring the entire counsel of God into the world of its time in order that its time might be transformed.[19]

Among the specific set of questions for the development of the theological vision that led to the successes at Redeemer are several that mirror those that govern my ministry:[20]

---

16. Eglinton, "Tim Keller and American Neo-Calvinism."

17. Elzinga, "Christian Higher Education," 11. "Christian higher education, to merit that designation and imprimatur, should be dominated by a faculty who are followers of Jesus. By that I mean the majority of faculty at an institution of Christian higher education should be Christians. The designation or description makes no sense if that is not the case."

18. Keller, *Center Church*, 17.

19. Lints, *Fabric of Theology*, 9.

20. Keller, *Center Church*, 18.

- What is the gospel and how do we bring it to bear on the hearts of people today?
- What is the culture like? How can we connect to it, challenge it, and communicate with it?
- How innovative must we be to reach people?
- How will we make the case to our people about the truth of Christianity?

MY THEOLOGICAL VISION

My theological vision is to build a culturally relevant bridge between biblical theology and science, such that my students can understand who they are in Christ. I want them to know that they are not, as the materialist posits, a random colocation of atoms but eternal souls, "fearfully and wonderfully made" (Ps 139:14), with beautifully designed and complex biochemical machines, made in the image and the likeness of God (Gen 1:27). I want them to be excited about life and their future because they understand that God has a plan for their lives (Ps 139:13–16), and that they have been put on this earth at this specific time for a specific purpose (Esth 4:14). I want to use science in both the classroom and the laboratory to help create an awareness of God's presence everywhere, visible or invisible (Col 1:16), such that they will learn how to be "surprised by Joy," as C. S. Lewis (1898–1963) wrote: "To attend, to come awake, remain receptive or run the risk of missing God who is everywhere incognito."[21] My vision for them is to become people for whom "Jesus Christ is preeminent."[22]

Solomon's words for the necessity of a vision are a serious reminder to those of us who are charged with the oversight of our students at Christian universities: "Where there is no prophetic vision the people cast off restraint, but blessed is he who keeps the law" (Prov 29:18).

21. Brown, *Life Observed*, 34.
22. Elzinga, "Christian Higher Education," 16.

SUMMARY

In this chapter we compared a university to a cultural center to establish a paradigm to help share the gospel effectively. We looked at three necessary characteristics of faculty at Christian universities: faith integration in the classroom, servant leadership, and mentorship. We suggested Timothy Keller's *Center Church* template as a model that professors can use to effectively bridge doctrine (orthodoxy) and ministry expression (orthopraxy) with theological vision. I explained in detail my own theological vision through which the gospel, in its proper cultural context, must be connected and communicated to a generation of young people, using innovative methodology tailored to a curriculum that makes the case for the truth of Christianity. In the chapters ahead, I will detail the various aspects of my methodology, developed over the last five years, to fruitfully reach my students with the gospel.

CHAPTER TWO

Know Their Stories

Our first job as teachers is to make sure that we learn our students, that we connect with them on a real level.

—JAMES FORD[1]

INTRODUCTION

IN THIS CHAPTER I will detail an assignment I use to encourage students to share their life journeys with me. This assignment is an important step in the realization of my theological vision for them as well as a way to teach them the importance of integrating their faith into what will become their future careers as nurses in a secular world. This exercise also allows me to get to know who my students are in a manner that is natural and not coercive. Gen Z loves writing about themselves; sharing details about their personal lives is something they do unabashedly. I have collected

---

1. Quoted in Sparks, "Teacher-Student Relationships Matter," para. 6. James Ford was the 2015 North Carolina State Teacher of the Year and the program director for the Public School Forum of North Carolina.

over one hundred of these essays, portions of which I will share in this chapter along with several important spiritual principles my students have themselves realized as they reflected on this assignment. I provide excerpts from the student essays to show the assignment's effectiveness in getting students to open up about themselves as well as end-of-course comments which show how our relationships grew.

WE NEED TO LIVE AMONG THE PEOPLE AND LEARN THEIR LANGUAGE

One of the first steps a minister must take when preparing to preach to his people is to know his congregation. Where do they come from? What have they gone through in their lives? Do they have a stable family situation? What are their dreams? Their fears? Their insecurities?[2] While these questions and concerns are directed to ministers, they are applicable to professors at Christian universities. We are ministers of the gospel to our "congregation." To be able to effectively mentor our students, we must first get to know them. Chapell adds, "We need to live among the people and know how to speak to them. We have to learn their language."[3]

It is almost impossible to know every student personally, especially at a large university. To ask personal questions directly, unless the result of student-initiated conversations, is improper and could be interpreted as inappropriate. Asking them to stand up in front of a room full of their peers and share their life stories would never be successful either, especially on the first day of class. I discovered several years ago, quite by accident, that this assignment, originally designed to teach my students how to organically integrate nursing with the gospel, provided them with

---

2. Compare the questions from Chapell, "Exploring New Listeners": "To whom are we talking in our congregations? What are the apologetic presuppositions in a post-modern era? Many of our students have lost confidence in the truth. The consequence is the loss of our youth even if they have been regular attenders in evangelical, Bible-believing churches."

3. Chapell, "Components and Process of Exposition."

the perfect opportunity to introduce themselves and share their life journeys in ways I never expected. Its success provides a model for other professors looking for an innovative way to get to know their students.

"A SISTERHOOD OF NURSES"

On the first day of every semester, I assign an extra-credit paper to all of my laboratory sections of pre-nursing students. They are asked to read "A Sisterhood of Nurses," an article that was published in the *Wall Street Journal* on Aug. 11, 2018.[4] The article follows the lives of six Filipino women who came to the US over forty years ago to live out the American dream by pursuing careers in nursing. They attended the same nursing school and, upon graduation, decided they would stay together. All six were hired by the Kansas City College of Osteopathic Medicine to work as a team. Their friendship continued to grow at a time when the field of medicine was becoming more difficult and demanding due to changes in technology. The demands of instrumentation made it difficult for these nurses to be personal with their patients; nevertheless, their love for nursing, compassion for their patients, and the support they gave to each other proved to be the winning formula. Despite several moving away, getting married and starting families, or assuming executive positions at other hospitals, the six women stayed in touch with each other.

This assignment has proven to be the key to unlock the doors to my students' hearts.

As pre-nursing students, the story of these six Filipino nurses who developed a lifelong friendship—a sisterhood—resonates with them at the stage in their lives when they are themselves looking to launch out in careers in nursing and hoping to develop similar lifelong friendships at college.

In the prompt for the assignment, students are asked to write a one-to-two-page summary of the article, identify at least one

---

4. Lagnado, "Sisterhood of Nurses."

biblical principle that the six women evidenced, supporting this with a reference from Scripture, and finally, write about themselves and their own faith journey. Gen Z loves to talk about themselves, especially their mental health.[5]

Many of my students are unafraid to share their own life journeys which include not just the banal details of where they are from and where they went to school, but also the tragedies, heartbreaks, and difficult family situations that have shaped them into the young people they are currently—and the nurses they will ultimately become. Many believe they were divinely called to study nursing at Palm Beach Atlantic University. Some are thinking about becoming nurses on the mission field. Not every story is pretty. I have read about a father's tragic death, a sister's attempted suicide, a student whose birth parents were only thirteen years old when she was born, or parents currently going through a bitter divorce. Many of these essays have led to follow-up conversations. A few have been transformational; for example, I have seen an atheist come to Christ.

THEY'RE DYING TO TELL US THEIR STORIES[6]

In this section I highlight a table of common themes from a total of 121 submissions, collected since the fall 2019 semester. Table 3 is followed by longer, unedited excerpts, used with permission.[7]

---

5. Cuncic, "Why Gen Z Is More Open."

6. The title of this section is an allusion to the elevated suicide rates among members of Generation Z. A least four students in my classes have at some point seriously contemplated taking their own lives. Rummo, "They're Dying to Tell You."

7. Students write these essays with the understanding that I may use excerpts anonymously in a future research project.

Table 3 Number of Students Sharing Common Essay Themes 2020–2023

Believe I am called to help others	25
Immediate family member suffered or died from a debilitating disease	17
Would like to become a missionary nurse	13
Student suffered debilitating illness or trauma	13
Wanted to be a nurse since childhood	8
Spiritual walk not where it should be	8
Parents divorced or separated	6
Came to PBA because of student-professor relationships	4
Would like to be a nurse in an underprivileged community or country	4
Comes from a single-parent family	3
Student or family member attempted suicide	3

"In the summer of 2021, I fell into a deep depression.... There came a time where I decided I was a burden for everyone in my life. It felt like I would stay this way forever. That was the night I attempted [suicide]."[8]

"I know I cannot do [nursing] in my own strength. God has gifted everyone with their own spiritual gifts, and I believe mine is to serve and care for others."

"I truly believe that God's purpose for putting me on this earth [is] to be a nurse and to take care of those who need it. I [hope to] go on trips throughout the world that need medical and spiritual help. I would love to go on a mission trip that involved medically helping a group of people while also spreading the Gospel."

---

8. This story has a happy ending. "That was the night I also realized I shouldn't have taken life for granted. From that day on I made a promise to myself that I would never let myself get to this point again so I turned back to God giving him 'another chance.' I later realized he never left my side. This was also when I decided to become a nurse. God taught me a lesson and kept me here to help people who are suffering."

"I have had hardships within my life and within my family that have made me feel the pain of wanting to be helped. My family has struggled with divorce and health problems."

"Recently, I have not been as close with the Lord, but I have had a new spark in my faith and am committed to getting closer to him."

"There are multiple places in the Bible where Jesus demonstrates his love by caring for others. I want to look like Jesus in the way that he cared [for others]."

"I cannot exactly remember when or why, but I remember having this feeling that there was more to life than what I had. From then on, I prayed to God every day, asking him to let me feel him in my heart, in my life, and this time I meant it."

"I am a strong believer in everything happening for a reason and that everything is a part of God's plan so I try and look at all medical issues I have experienced that will only make me better at my job because I can relate to what patients are feeling."

"When I was [four] years old, my parents got divorced. I had the privilege to watch my mom get out of a poor marriage that . . . did not reflect a biblical marriage. I watched her become healed and then remarry my stepdad that I am now proud to call my dad. Sometimes I wish he was my biological father to begin with."

"God has given me a heart for caring for others and their well-being in all aspects. . . . God told us we would experience trials and difficulties in the world but because he has overcome the world, we can find strength in him in order to get through these difficult times."

"I chose to become a nurse because I have a passion for God's people and the degree of complexity to which he designed them. The pairing of these two serves as a way for me to fall more in love with the creator while loving his people and building relationships with people that need support in a vulnerable time. Excellent healthcare is a great [demonstration] of Jesus' love because of the selflessness and sacrifice it requires."

Many of the responses I have received over the last four years have fallen into definable categories or general truths about life.

These were showcased in an essay I wrote for *Christian Scholar's Review*.[9] Several excerpts appear below.

HAPPINESS COMES FROM SERVING OTHERS

One of my male nursing students whose decision to attend PBA was largely based on our "offer of faith-based classes" wrote, "My interest in nursing is the fact that I can make someone's day better, save someone's life or even just comfort someone in a scary situation. I learned that my happiness comes from making someone's day just that much better or even seeing a smile on their face." Many of us have heard something similar preached from the pulpit: If you want to get out of your funk, then go and do something nice for someone else. We are wired for happiness. True joy is initially found when a person surrenders his life to Christ. After that, the Christian will be most happy when serving others sacrificially. Another student wrote, "I want to show Christ's love through my service," echoing the words of Jesus: "The greatest among you will be your servant" (Matt 23:11).

DIFFICULT CIRCUMSTANCES ARE NOT AN EXCUSE TO PLAY THE VICTIM CARD

There are many examples of people in the Bible who, despite being raised in either dysfunctional families or enduring unexpected tragedies, refused to allow their circumstances to become their identity. Jacob ran for his life from his brother Esau. Joseph's jealous brothers attempted to murder him by throwing him down a well. Naomi's husband and two sons died unexpectedly. We do not get to decide where or to whom we are born nor to dictate the circumstances we face in early childhood. Several of my students have come from broken homes where they experienced abuse, or their parents went through a bitter divorce resulting in their being raised in single-parent homes. Notwithstanding, they have

---

9. Rummo, "What Nursing Students Can Teach."

decided not to become victims. One wrote, "I am a first-generation college student in my family. Growing up, my mom was a single mom with two kids. I learned how to earn things if I wanted them. Also, never to take anything for granted. Most importantly, I learned how to grind to get to where I want to go." Another wrote, "When I was little my mom went to nursing school despite being a single parent, which was already tough. Her passion and care towards others inspired me to do the same." These two young ladies recognized that despite their less-than-ideal circumstances, God is sovereign in their lives, and they have chosen to be victors instead of victims.

GOD USES TRAGEDY TO DRIVE US TO OUR PURPOSE

In Isa 61, the Lord promises Israel to "appoint unto them that mourn in Zion, to give unto them beauty for ashes, the oil of joy for mourning, the garment of praise for the spirit of heaviness; that they might be called trees of righteousness, the planting of the LORD, that he might be glorified" (Isa 61:3 KJV).

This promise was especially comforting to one of my Jewish students whose essay recounted several family tragedies.

> [My father] was a gentle, beautiful man but mentally ill. My family suffered tremendously after he took his life... [then] my younger sister was diagnosed with cancer... the chemotherapy made her violently ill every day. The only people who could ever brighten her dark days were the nurses.... I want to be that person those nurses were for my sister.

Another student wrote about her brother who "was [born an invalid] and diagnosed with spastic quadriplegia cerebral palsy, epilepsy and an array of other [diseases]." She went on to recount that her life was continually surrounded by medical equipment and home nurses. As she grew, she learned from them, "I could easily name [my brother's] conditions and... even the medications taken." As a result, she has always wanted to go into the medical field, but she chose nursing because the doctors rarely acknowledged her. She shared,

> The nurses often said "Hi," asked if I wanted anything and even tried to memorize my name. These small interactions had a significant impact on my life. The nurses became role models for me by seeing how they cared for my brother and would work tirelessly to make him comfortable. I aspire to do this for other medically complex children and as a result, I hope I can be a friendly face to those siblings painfully watching their siblings suffer.

Her brother passed away in May, 2018. She has not returned to the hospitals that took care of him. Although she says it will be difficult to work in an environment that will bring back difficult memories, "I do believe that [nursing] is my God-given calling."

THE IMPORTANT THINGS IN LIFE ARE OFTEN CAUGHT, NOT TAUGHT

"My mom is a nurse, and she loves what she does," wrote one student. "The way [she] cares for others and shows kindness really inspires me to want to be like her." Another wrote, "I was especially in awe of the nurses. I would ask them questions and feel my nerves go away from talking to them. I would tell my mom, 'I want to do what they do when I am older.'"

In the classic book *Spiritual Leadership*, J. Oswald Sanders notes, "The power of inspiring others to service and sacrifice will mark God's leader. Such a leader is a light for others around."[10] Sanders's words serve as a reminder to professors at Christian universities that we have the privilege and the responsibility to inspire our students to serve and sacrifice. But we have to get to know them to do this effectively. The apostle Paul reminds us, "Join together in following my example, brothers and sisters, and just as

---

10. Sanders, *Spiritual Leadership*, 67.

you have us as a model, keep your eyes on those who live as we do" (Phil 3:17).

The Bible reminds us, "Not many of you should become teachers, my brothers, for you know that we who teach will be judged with greater strictness" (Jas 3:1). Scripture teaches that we face greater accountability. That may not be encouraging, and it may even be a little frightening if a professor is contemplating a career in Christian academia. But to those of us who are here already, we are needed now more than ever to help those students dealing with pain to see God's hand in it.

SUMMARY

Getting to know my students is the first step in being able to effectively serve and mentor them. I have been able to accomplish this with the unique assignment described in this chapter. Professors teaching in other disciplines would do well to implement a similar strategy, unique to the subject they teach. When students write about themselves, it makes them feel like their professor cares for them as individuals, and does not treat them as names on a student roster.

This assignment has afforded opportunities for follow-up conversations. I include them here as a kind of "proof concept," to emphasize this point about how students feel when their professors reach out to them personally.

"I can't express enough how much your interest in my story about my sister meant to me. I don't get to be vulnerable with my professors very often and it means a lot that you wanted to know more."

"Never did I think I would be upset about ending chemistry class with you, but I wanted to thank you for never giving up on me. I appreciate you more than you know. Thank you for checking in [on] me and always being someone I can joke around with. There are few professors you can do that with. Some of your mannerisms are like my father's, a tough mentality but a loving heart. Again, I want to thank you for being a light in my life. Have a great summer, enjoy the time with your wife and family. I'm blessed you are a part of my journey."

The assignment presented in this chapter is an extremely effective tool in helping to create a relationship with my students. The response rate to this assignment is over 90 percent. The willingness of the students to share their personal lives and the transparency with which they do so is an important first step to reach them effectively with the gospel. But this is just the first step. In the next chapter, I'll explain the importance of developing an ethos of hospitality which will allow you to build on this relationship with your students.

CHAPTER THREE

Developing an Ethos of "Extravagant" and "Intentional" Hospitality[1]

Be hospitable to one another without complaint.

—1 Pet 4:9

INTRODUCTION

IN THIS CHAPTER I will discuss the importance of exhibiting an ethos[2] of "extravagant and intentional" hospitality as the means to deepen relationships with my students. The ideas in this chapter took root several years ago when a group of students showed up at my office door for help with chemistry homework. We spent several hours together solving problems on a large whiteboard on

1. Richter and Miller, "How to Feed Gen Z's Hunger."
2. Chapell, *Christ-Centered Preaching*, 26. Chapell explains that Aristotle's *logos*, *pathos*, and *ethos* are all necessary when ministering the gospel. In modern parlance, if we're not walking the walk, no one will listen to our talk. If we wish to reach our students with the gospel, our love and testimony have to be manifest.

the wall behind my desk. I thought it would be a good idea to put together a tray of snacks for them for supplemental brain sugar. Word quickly got out and more students began showing up for "homework help." On several occasions I had as many as seven students, crammed around my desk, sitting on the floor or just outside the door, craning their necks to follow along. My office has now become a place for more than just chemistry tutoring. It has been dubbed the "chill zone." It is the place where students can grab a snack, a free book, a cup of coffee, engage in casual conversation, ask me for life hacks, or drop in for prayer. Sometimes they come just to pray for me. Accidentally, and then intentionally, I have sought to make my office a place of hospitality.

From Abraham to Jesus, our ultimate model, the Bible is full of characters who showed hospitality.[3] The lesson—taught implicitly and explicitly in Scripture—is that God's people should do likewise. Demonstrating biblical hospitality is not a suggestion. Scripture commands that Christians show hospitality to the saints, strangers, and, I might add, to our students—who are, after all, our neighbors.[4]

To make my argument, I will first define what the Bible teaches about hospitality, what this means in practice to those of us who teach at Christian universities, and how I demonstrate hospitality to my students in meaningful ways.

WHAT IS BIBLICAL HOSPITALITY?

When one thinks of hospitality, it is almost always accompanied by mental images of Martha Stewart or the concierge stand at a Marriott resort. That's actually not far from one New Testament definition. The Greek word *philoxenia* (lit., lover of strangers) is a term

---

3. Klein, "Ultimate Guide to Christian Hospitality."
4. "But when you give a reception, invite the poor, the crippled, the lame, the blind, and you will be blessed, since they do not have the means to repay you" (Luke 14:13–14). "Do not neglect to show hospitality to strangers, for by this some have entertained angels without knowing it" (Heb. 13:2). "But hospitable, loving what is good, sensible, just, devout, self-controlled" (Titus 1:8).

for hospitality meaning to receive a stranger as a guest. A second Greek word, *xenodocheo* (lit., *xenos*, "stranger," and *dechomai*, "take with the hand, receive, accept"),[5] is used by Paul in a list of godly characteristics of a deserving widow: "if she has . . . shown hospitality" (1 Tim 5:10). Here the word has the added concept of extending hands and accepting a marginalized person into one's home.[6]

The Old Testament emphasizes the concept of the stranger or the foreigner. It was forbidden by Mosaic law that "the seed of the righteous" be left "begging for bread" (Ps 37:25; cf. Exod 22:22; 23:9), and so most instances of hospitality were extended to aliens and strangers. In Judaism, showing hospitality to guests is considered a *mitzvah*: a command or an obligation.[7]

Henri J. M. Nouwen (1932-1996) writes, "[Hospitality] is one of the richest biblical terms that can deepen and broaden our insight in our relationships to fellow human beings."[8] Even more, Garwood Anderson, dean of Nashotah House and professor of New Testament at Marquette University, explains that all hospitality originates from God:

> Hospitality in its biblical context is shaped by the beneficent character of God. It reflects his saving acts and is regulated by divine instruction. One reason that the people of Israel must treat aliens and strangers with hospitality is that Israel experienced being strangers and aliens in Egypt (Exod 22:21; 23:9; Lev 19:33-34; Deut 10:19; 24:17-18; see also Jer 7:5-7). Another reason to practice hospitality is that Yahweh cares for aliens and strangers (Pss 39:12; 68:6; 146:9) and his people should share his concern.[9]

---

5. Foley, "Prevenient Grace."

6. "Extending Hands" is one of Palm Beach Atlantic's core values so this definition is especially pertinent to my ministry.

7. Jewish Virtual Library, "Hospitality."

8. Nouwen, *Reaching Out*, 47.

9. Anderson, *Hospitality*, 40.

Broadly speaking then, hospitality is the "quality or disposition of receiving and treating guests and strangers in a warm, friendly, generous way."[10]

FROM THEN TO NOW: BIBLICAL HOSPITALITY TODAY

The definition of hospitality is especially appropriate for my students, most of whom are freshmen and away from home for the first time. Some are homesick. In a sense, they are strangers in a foreign land, and often in need of a friendly place where they can experience genuine hospitality.

It is impossible to look at the word *hospitality* and not recognize the idea of a *hospital* at its root. In fact, Latin takes us there: The words *hospitality* and *hospital* are both derived from the Latin *hospes*, uniting both Old and New Testament concepts. In this vein, *biblical hospitality* is the demonstration of obedient, compassionate action towards strangers, using our means to meet the needs of those less fortunate than ourselves.[11]

Pastors Kyle Richter and Patrick Miller co-wrote an article for the Gospel Coalition in which they offer five suggestions for how to feed Gen Z's hunger for Jesus. One of them is by offering "extravagant hospitality."

> From the first time a college student enters our doors to the day he or she moves away, we're extravagantly and intentionally hospitable. We smile when we greet people. We learn their names. We immediately connect them with insiders. We follow up after they leave. We let them know we miss them if they haven't shown up for a while.

10. Byma, "Hospitality and Nursing," para. 1.
11. Pohl, *Making Room*. "The biblical meaning of hospitality—making room for the stranger, especially those in most acute need. Such care must not be reduced to mere social entertaining nor may it be self-interested and reciprocal; instead, biblical hospitality reaches out to the abject and lowly and expects nothing in return. Hospitality is not optional, nor should it be understood as a rare spiritual gift; instead, it is a normative biblical practice that is learned by doing it." Gushee, "Making Room," para. 3.

DEVELOPING AN ETHOS OF HOSPITALITY

We train leaders to invite students into their homes for meals. After spending over a year isolated during a global lockdown, Gen Z is hungry for the hospitality Jesus showed to sinners, disciples, and Pharisees alike. His ministry was a movable feast, breaking cultural norms—ask the woman who cleaned his feet with her tears—so he could communicate a deep truth through action: *God wants you at his table too.*[12]

The first miracle of Jesus' ministry pointed to this kind of hospitality. This first miracle occurred at a wedding feast. John, the gospel writer, added that the *miracle* of transforming water into wine was also a *sign*, a portent of Jesus' ministry to follow: "This, the first of his signs, Jesus did at Cana in Galilee, and manifested his glory. And his disciples believed in him" (John 2:11).[13] Jesus wants all people at his table. Richter and Miller emphasize that it is the older generation's responsibility to get involved in reaching out to Gen Z, explaining that it's not just a free meal they want but also "mentoring relationships."[14]

Likewise, Abigail Thompson asks the reader to "reimagine hospitality":

> What if it wasn't about creating the perfect environment for entertaining but about making our homes purposeful for the kingdom? What if, instead of hiding from a broken world, we invited the broken in? This is how we make

---

12. Richter and Miller, "How to Feed Gen Z's Hunger," paras. 10–11.

13. Keller, *Prodigal God*, 120. "Amazingly, John, the gospel writer calls this miracle a 'sign,' a signifier of what Jesus's ministry was all about. Why would this be his inaugural act? Why would Jesus, to convey what he had come to do, choose to turn 150 gallons of water into superb wine in order to keep a party going? The answer is that Jesus came to bring festival joy. He is the real, true 'Master of the Banquet,' the Lord of the feast."

14. Richter and Miller, "How to Feed Gen Z's Hunger," para. 12. "Older saints must be challenged not to simply retire but to use their freed-up time to pass down the good deposit of the gospel to future generations. This can happen formally through mentoring programs or by encouraging older church members to lead small groups for young people. But it can also happen informally on Sunday morning, at coffee meetups, or through an invitation to lunch."

the gospel real to the loneliest generation on earth.[15] It's not an overstatement to suggest that Christians opening their homes and inviting young people into their lives could transform a generation. We have a God who sets the lonely in families (Ps 68:6). All we need to do is make room.[16]

Hospitality is not some stuffy, outdated practice.[17] If we want to be able to minister to our students outside of the classroom, we have to treat them like family. If we want them to listen to us when we speak to them about the gospel, we have to earn the right.

As Willis and Clements memorably put it, "[Hospitality] is the Gospel with flesh on."[18] God extends hospitality to humanity from Genesis to Revelation. He created a home for Adam and Eve in a lush garden, and he will create a city—the New Jerusalem—for believers as our final home (Rev 21). If hospitality is so important to God, then it must be practiced as "the primary way we tell the astounding story that God hasn't given up on us. Any time we practice hospitality, we follow in the steps of our lavishly hospitable God."[19]

How then can Christian faculty model this same ethos of hospitality to students?

What follows is a list of practical suggestions to create an atmosphere of hospitality. Although most of the following are specifically related to the school office, faculty must work to develop an ethos of hospitality, remembering that the goal is gospel advancement through "care and healing—we do the caring and Jesus does the healing."[20]

15. Jenkins, "3 Things."
16. Thompson, "Gen Z Needs a Place," para. 10.
17. Willis and Clements, *Simplest Way*, 40.
18. Willis and Clements, *Simplest Way*, 40–41.
19. Willis and Clements, *Simplest Way*, 42.
20. Willis and Clements, *Simplest Way*, 70.

DEVELOPING AN ETHOS OF HOSPITALITY

1. Order: Maintain an office characterized by logos, not chaos, thus reflecting the divine order of the creation.

After reading *The Benedict Option* by Rod Dreher, I thought about the changes I could make to my school office that would allow me to reach my students more effectively for Christ. Dreher writes, "If we don't have internal order we will be controlled by our human passions and by the powerful outside forces who are in greater control of directing liquid modernity's deep currents."[21] As a chemistry professor, I am most at home discussing the *logos*—the divine order of the cosmos that characterizes God's handiwork in the creation. I saw the need for my office to reflect the character of the world I taught about.

My office is a museum. There is glassware and molecular models of oligopeptides and nucleic acids on the shelves and windowsill where a Chinese elm bonsai reaches up towards heaven, its delicate green leaves giving praise to its Creator from beneath two bright grow lights. The walls are lined with framed newspaper articles I have written and color photographs I have taken of tropical waterbirds in the lakes behind our south Florida home. A periodic table of the elements, a photograph of Albert Einstein (1879–1955), a right brain/left brain piece of art, and photos from missionary trips I have been on over the years surround a large whiteboard that is always covered with equations, reactions, or solved problems from students' homework. Across from my desk, nailed to a wall pillar, are two plaques; one reads, "Climb Every Mountain," and the other, "It's Not About You—to God be the Glory." A celestial star globe sits on a high shelf next to a humorous caricature of me. Over my doorway hangs a painting of the scene of the throne of God from Isa 6 that my older daughter painted shortly after our move to Florida in 2017, when I was struggling to adjust after leaving behind in New Jersey our family and friends for over thirty years. I always enjoy observing students who, the first time in my office, sit in one of my two visitor's chairs and allow their eyes to wander. Inevitably, something sparks a conversation,

---

21. Rod Dreher, *Benedict Option*, 3.

often aided by my diffuser, its vapors gently wafting towards the ceiling; a liturgy in its own rite, especially when the oil is frankincense. The eclectic adornment of my office is designed by intention. It is a reflection of God's intelligent design. God just didn't *make* life. He *created* life. His creation was artful, beautiful, and complex. There is beauty to be seen everywhere. Dreher writes, "You never know how God will use the little things in a life ordered by His love, to His service, to speak evangelically to others. . . . Everything is evangelical. Everything is directed to God. Everything has to be seen from the supernatural point of view. The radiance that comes through our lives is only a reflection of God."[22]

2. Prayer: Engage with your students prayerfully and pray with them often.

It is important to be great educators in the Christian tradition by integrating faith into the classes we teach. But there's more to it than starting class off with a prayer. I do begin almost every class with a prayer that includes praying for my students to learn and for me to be clear in my lecture. But prayer doesn't end in the classroom. When students come to my office for whatever reason—whether help with a difficult assignment, to review an exam, to discuss a research project, a personal issue, or just an emotional meltdown—they know that my office is a sanctuary, a "chill zone" as one of my students has characterized it, where they can come and share whatever it is that is on their minds or hearts. I make it a habit to pray with them before they leave, a tradition that has sometimes resulted in moist eyes.

---

22. Dreher, *Benedict Option*, 57.

3. *Work: "Can become very transformative—and very prayerful too."*[23]

Work is a word that some students dislike. No—they actually find it anathema. In science, this attitude is the quickest way to a change in major. Pinned on my corkboard is a copy of a *New York Times* article titled "Why Science Majors Change Their Minds (It's Just So Darn Hard)."[24] The headline alone serves as a reminder to students entering my office that they need to commit to four years of hard work, which means not just reading countless textbook pages but lots of pencil pushing across scrap paper, as well as time spent in the laboratory. An opinion piece I wrote in 2021, titled "10 Suggestions for Incoming College STEM Freshmen," contained this as one of the ten suggestions for success in STEM courses: "My college physics teacher had a cartoon on his office door that showed a confused student explaining to his professor that he really understood the material, he just couldn't do the problems. You cannot learn science by osmosis. Magic happens when the brain, eyes and hand all come together in beautiful synaptic choreography, guiding a pencil across a sheet of paper."[25] When students come to my office for help, it's time to roll up their sleeves. And I often ask them to take out a pencil and a piece of paper even if they are working on an online assignment on their laptop or tablet. Helping students in their labor is an important part of demonstrating hospitality. If they are struggling to understand a difficult concept that I might not have explained clearly in one of my lectures, or if they need a nudge in the right direction to get started on a homework assignment, this is meaningful to them since it directly impacts their grade.

---

23. Dreher, *Benedict Option*, 62.
24. Drew, "Why Science Majors Change."
25. Rummo, "10 Suggestions."

4. Stability: My office is a place where students can find stability.

I like to think my office is a place where students can come and feel settled. It was only two years ago that we climbed out of a years-long pandemic that impacted students' lives in ways we are still learning about. The majority of my students are first-year students, and my assumption is always that they spent two or three semesters in high school sitting home behind computer screens, attempting to finish their sophomore and junior years as best as they could. They now need stability and structure in their lives. Yes, they are in college and they are supposed to be adults. But I know better. My wife and I have raised four children: two sons now in their thirties and two adopted Chinese daughters who are both Gen Zers and attend the university where I teach. I know what my girls went through and they, like many of my students, need help finding their way.

5. Community: "A feeling of fellowship with others, as a result of sharing common attitudes, interests, and goals."[26]

Anyone teaching at a Christian university knows that it is a community. But the idea of community must extend beyond the classroom and the office hours mandated by a course syllabus.

Here are a few simple suggestions to extend the idea of community among students in a meaningful way. In my experience, they'll catch these and appreciate them.

- Attend chapel and make it a part of your weekly schedule. Our campus pastor tells me that students notice which professors attend chapel regularly.[27]

---

26. Google Dictionary, from Oxford Languages, "community (*n.*), sense 2," accessed Oct. 23, 2024.

27. I continue to be embarrassed by the poor attendance of faculty to chapel on my campus and the excuses some have made. Students are watching. They know which faculty members value chapel. Chapel is one of the most important aspects at a Christian university that establishes its culture.

- Eat lunch with your students in the dining hall.
- If one of your students invites you to attend a sporting event in which he or she is on the team, show up.
- Encourage your students to attend a doctrinally sound church where they can get involved serving. The best way to accomplish this is to be involved yourself at your church, perhaps teaching a small group, serving on the welcome team, or singing in the choir.
- Look for opportunities to participate in an off-campus university-sponsored work opportunity as a volunteer with a student group.
- Lead a mission trip.[28]
- Consider inviting a group of students to your home for a meal.
- When the "Big Red Bus" pulls up on campus, roll up your sleeves and donate blood, then encourage students to join you. I can't think of a more appropriate illustration of the gospel than giving one's own blood so that another person can live.[29]

6. Sustenance for the mind and body: Make snacks, coffee, and good books available.

My syllabi list official office hours but I always add, "anytime my door is open, and my light is on, feel free to drop in for *whatever*." Once my students find out that I have a tray with a generous variety of salty and sweet snacks, they take me up on it (as do a number of my professorial colleagues). My wife goes to great lengths to

---

28. On this point, see chapter 7.
29. "Small Act, Big Impact. Every person has the power to save a life. Donating blood only takes a little of your time, and it can mean a lifetime for patients in need." Banner on home page, accessed Oct. 17, 2024, oneblood.org.

keep my inventory well-stocked with chips and cookies. It is an inexpensive way to make students feel welcome.

But it's not just about food. Several years ago, I began a program to purchase Christian books in bulk that I thought would be helpful to students depending on where they were in their spiritual walk. *Don't Waste Your Life* by John Piper was among my first offerings. For students planning to go on a mission trip I purchased copies of *Eternity in their Hearts* by Don Richardson. And for any anxious members of Gen Z, *The Freedom of Self-Forgetfulness* by Timothy Keller is a great read. These can be purchased at reasonable prices from online book distributors. Some publishers offer faculty corporate account status, allowing the purchase of books at a significant discount.

7. Balance: "Prudence, mercy and good judgment."[30]

The Benedictine monks define balance as being Christ-like in all things while fulfilling the Lord's calling. It doesn't matter whether a person is called to a secular or a sacred life; the Bible makes no distinction between the two. Our students need to see this type of balance in our lives. The only great tragedy in life according to Dreher is that "no matter what a Christian's circumstances, he cannot live faithfully if God is only part of his life, bracketed away from the rest. In the end, either Christ is at the center of our lives or the Self and all its idolatries. There is no middle ground."[31]

8. Attentiveness: Be actively involved in the student's mental health.

As I wrote at the beginning of this chapter, it is impossible to look at the word *hospitality* and not recognize the idea of a *hospital* at its root. The incidences of depression, anxiety, suicides, and overall

---

30. Dreher, *Benedict Option*, 63.
31. Dreher, *Benedict Option*, 74.

mental crises have reached an all-time high among young children and teenagers.[32] The second highest cause of death among teens after accidents is suicide. In light of these bleak statistics, faculty must make themselves available to talk about mental health with our students. Our university recently hosted a mental health seminar to train members of the PBA community to become "young-mental-health first-aiders." Attendees learned how to recognize and deal with the signs of mental health struggles among students including anxiety, depression, threats of violence to themselves or others, and thoughts of suicide. This is an issue that every faculty member at Christian universities should be concerned with, especially since they are the ones who spend the most time throughout the week in the classroom with students and can observe changes in behavior and performance.

SUMMARY[33]

In this chapter I suggested numerous ways to demonstrate hospitality to students by creating a welcoming atmosphere in my school office. This is an important next step in continuing to develop mentoring relationships that lead to gospel conversations with students. But hospitality is not limited to an office. Professors at Christian colleges must be known as people who love their students, are interested in them as individuals and not just names on a roster, and are willing to become involved in their lives outside of the classroom. Teaching the subjects in our fields of expertise with passion and excellent pedagogy is our calling: "In everything

---

32. Petersen, "Rise in Suicides by Young Children," para. 4. "The number of children dying by suicide has risen dramatically in recent years. Parents often don't know that their children are having suicidal thoughts, new research shows. Among females ages 10 to 14, the rate of suicide more than tripled between 2007 and 2020, from 0.5 per 100,000 to 2 per 100,000 according to data from the National Center for Health Statistics. Among males the same age, the rate jumped from 1.2 per 100,000 to 3.6 per 100,000 over the same period."

33. The associate provost at PBA asked me to put together a presentation for faculty on hospitality for a breakout session during faculty week at the start of the fall 2022 semester.

set them an example by doing what is good. In your teaching show integrity, seriousness" (Titus 2:7 NIV). But pointing the way to God for students so that they may be transformed into the likeness of his son, Jesus Christ, requires that we develop an ethos of "extravagant" and "intentional" hospitality. In the next chapter I will explain the importance of teaching students how to integrate their faith with current issues in the health sciences and how I go about this in my chemistry classes.

CHAPTER FOUR

Integrating Faith in the Chemistry Classroom

And Jehovah God formed man of the dust of the ground, and breathed into his nostrils the breath of life; and man became a living soul.

—Gen 2:7 (ASV)

INTRODUCTION

THE PREVIOUS CHAPTERS HAVE focused primarily on how I go about fulfilling the second part of PBA's motto, "enriching souls."[1] In this chapter I will describe my approach to "enlightening the minds" of my students by awakening in them an understanding of the *imago Dei*. It can be as simple as playing a classic seventies soft-rock song while they filter into the classroom and then briefly

---

1. The full motto is "enlightening minds, enriching souls, and extending hands."

discussing it; a response to a post;[2] or a written essay on a current event in the field of health, social, or pure science where they have an opportunity to integrate a biblical worldview. Our road map for this chapter begins by showing how the Bible and science are not mutually exclusive, how the *imago Dei* is defined, and how God is everywhere present but we must look for him. I then share examples of student essays on a variety of social and pure science topics where they have successfully integrated faith with science. The chapter closes with examples of faith integrations from seventies soft-rock songs that I often play for students before class begins and X (formerly Twitter) posts on a wide range of topics with which they can interact.

THE BIBLE AND SCIENCE—THE "ULTIMATE POWER COUPLE"[3]

The great scientists of the centuries leading up to the nineteenth century, before the advent of the "four bearded god-killers,"[4] were almost all Christians. It is noteworthy that the father of classical physics, Sir Isaac Newton (1643–1727), and the father of quantum physics, Max Planck (1858–1947), were both able to seamlessly integrate faith and science. Belief in God did not present a contradiction to their understanding of the design and the mechanics governing the respective worlds they studied. They both believed that God is the ultimate designer, "For in him all things were created: things in heaven and on earth, visible and invisible. . . . He is before all things, and in him all things hold together" (Col 1:16–17).

---

2. This past year I began to utilize X (formerly Twitter) in my courses. There is a short section about this later in this chapter.

3. Guillen, "Bible and Science."

4. Marty, "Freud and Other 'God-Killers.'" "Darwin-Marx-Nietzsche-Freud—dubbable, and sometimes dubbed, 'the four bearded god-killers' who framed now-classic, career-long attacks on God and gods and religion and religions, enjoy and suffer successions of varying critical fates."

The faith of these scientists motivated them to pursue the study of science. They had a biblical worldview, anchored in the Judeo-Christian tradition. They saw a world that was ordered and concluded that "nature had been designed by the same rational mind who had designed the human mind."[5] As Holmes Rolston explains,

> It was monotheism that launched the coming of physical sciences, for it premised an intelligible world, sacred but disenchanted, a world with a blueprint, which was therefore open to the searches of the scientists. The great pioneers in physics—Newton, Galileo, Kepler, Copernicus—devoutly believed themselves called to find evidences of God in the physical world.[6]

The seventeenth-century astronomer Johannes Kepler (1571–1630) said that "God wanted us to recognize natural laws and that God made this possible by creating us after his own image so that we could share in his own thoughts."[7] They understood human reason was a gift from a rational God, but they also believed that men were sinners, and this affected their ideas as well.[8] Thus, Steve Fuller argues,

> It was these two biblical ideas that were crucial to the rise of science, both of which can be attributed to the reading of Genesis provided by Augustine . . . whose work became increasingly studied in the late Middle Ages and especially the Reformation. Augustine captured two ideas in two Latin coinages . . . *imago Dei* and *peccatum originis*. The former says that humans are unique as a species in our having been created in the image and likeness of God, while the latter says that all

---

5. Meyer, *Return of the God Hypothesis*, 24.
6. Rolston, *Science and Religion*, 39.
7. Kepler to Herwart von Hohenberg, Apr. 9/10, 1599, in *Johannes Kepler, Life and Letters*, 50.
8. Meyer, *Return of the God Hypothesis*, 25.

humans are born having inherited the legacy of Adam's error, "original sin."⁹

Lydia Jaeger, the academic dean at the Institut Biblique de Nogent-sur-Marne in France, writes, "The doctrine of creation was influential in the birth of modern science. Why then should Christian theology have no resource to offer science today? . . . Theology draws on the Word of the very same God who created the world that science explores."¹⁰ It is this realization of God's creation and the *imago Dei* that I wish to awaken in my students by creating "God awareness" in lecture and laboratory classes. It is critical that they see the reciprocal nature of theology and science and the connection of both to creation.

Many of my students have been homeschooled or attended Christian high schools, and already have a rudimentary understanding of, and are interested to study further, the complementary relationship of faith and science. This is not surprising based on the latest research on Gen Z that has found it is the most accepting generation to faith's place at the table alongside science.

> Gen Z (57%, ages 16–24) [is] more likely to think religion has a place in the modern world than any other generation, whilst having a better understanding and greater acceptance of science. This compares to less than half of Millennials (47%, ages 25–40) and Gen X (47%, ages 41–56). The data also revealed that 37% of Gen Z think science and religion are compatible, compared with only 30% of the British public and 26% of Gen Xers.¹¹

CREATING GOD-AWARENESS—REAWAKENING THE *IMAGO DEI*

Back in the seventies when I was in college, pop culture had co-opted a quotation from Carl Sagan (1934–1996) that "we are

---

9. Fuller, "Foreword," 30.
10. Jaeger, "Science and Theology as Gifts," 10.
11. ISCAST, "Study Suggests That Gen Z," para. 1.

stardust."[12] Joni Mitchell echoed this theme and Crosby, Stills, and Nash embellished it in the song "Woodstock."[13] Another seventies song writer, Kerry Livgren from the group Kansas, explored this theme in his song "Dust in the Wind."[14] We did come from dust and "unto dust shall [we] return" (Gen 3:19 ASV). Nevertheless, the Bible is clear that we are not just a random colocation of atoms of simple elements from the stars, or even the larger molecules that make up the complex biochemistry that powers our life force. As we learn more about the inner workings of the cell and the complexity of molecular biology, it is becoming increasingly difficult to make the case that we are the product of random, unguided processes.

The *imago Dei* is what sets humans apart from all other created beings. It is the "metaphysical expression, associated uniquely to humans, which signifies the symbolical connection between God and humanity."[15] Simply stated, it means we reflect God. When we say that man was created in the image of God, we are recognizing that human nature consists of special qualities that God uses to carry out his plans and purposes.[16]

God breathed a living soul into the first man, making it possible for all of Adam's descendants to know the one, true God (Gen 2:7). This awareness is just the beginning. We are capable of a deeper knowledge of God through a personal relationship when we believe in his Son and then we are able to comprehend deeper, spiritual truths through his Spirit (e.g., 1 Cor 2). While those who have not heard the gospel have an awareness of someone greater outside our own dimension, I am hoping that the assignments presented in these chapters will point my students to the one true God who is everywhere present—and ultimately to the gospel.

12. Berkowitz, "On the Origins."
13. Mitchell, "Woodstock."
14. Livgren, "Dust in the Wind."
15. Christianity.com, "What Does '*Imago Dei*' Mean?," para. 1.
16. Christianity.com, "What Does '*Imago Dei*' Mean?"

GOD IS EVERYWHERE PRESENT: WE MUST LOOK FOR HIM UNTIL WE FIND HIM

King David wrote in Ps 139 that God is present everywhere:

> Where can I go from your Spirit?
> Where can I flee from your presence?
> If I go up to the heavens, you are there;
> if I make my bed in the depths, you are there.
> If I rise on the wings of the dawn,
> if I settle on the far side of the sea,
> even there your hand will guide me,
> your right hand will hold me fast.
> If I say, "Surely the darkness will hide me
> and the light become night around me,"
> even the darkness will not be dark to you;
> the night will shine like the day,
> for darkness is as light to you.
> (Ps 139:7–12)

Despite God being present everywhere, not all are *God-aware*. In many cases, God-awareness has to be taught. C. S. Lewis wrote, "One must learn to remember, to attend, to come awake, remain receptive, or run the risk of missing God who is everywhere incognito."[17] It behooves Christian educators to be observant for opportunities to see God's hand in unexpected places and then share these glimpses of the *imago Dei* with students through intentional faith integration in the classroom.

I teach several first-year chemistry courses.[18] About two-thirds of my students are in the university's nursing program and the other one-third are majoring in a variety of disciplines including biology, chemistry, pharmacy, forensic science, and pre-health.

---

17. Brown, *Life Observed*, 34.

18. I have taught four different chemistry courses to the two cohorts of students: Principles of General, Organic, and Biochemistry lecture with a laboratory component to the pre-nursing cohort, and Introduction to General Chemistry lecture, General Chemistry I, and General Chemistry II laboratory. Each class presents different opportunities for specific course-related faith integrations. I will share how I handle this in the laboratory sections in the next chapter.

Such a wide range of majors affords me endless opportunities to point to glimpses of God in creation, often in the most unexpected places.

In chapter 2, I wrote about the method I utilize in my pre-nursing class that allows me to get to know my students. There is another reason why I give this assignment. It is a prelude to what they can expect during the semester with additional extra credit opportunities on a range of topics which will be discussed in detail later in this chapter. Sometimes I introduce these topics in class and we briefly discuss them. More often, they are assigned as essays for extra credit towards upcoming exams. In my pre-nursing chemistry class, the topics are chosen to be relevant to their future careers in the medical field. In the other cohort, the topics I choose are more relevant to chemistry as a pure science. In both cases, the students are asked to read an article from a secular source and apply biblical critical thinking. I want them searching for glimpses of God in unexpected places until he is found—and he always is, even if it takes some work.

In the next sections, I will highlight several of these articles and showcase some students' responses. Also included at the end of this chapter is a brief list of seventies soft-rock songs and selected posts that I have shared with the students to spark conversations about their meaning in light of science, the gospel, and often both.

FAITH INTEGRATION IN CHEMISTRY AS A PURE SCIENCE

Since both cohorts are studying chemistry, there are several topics that are congruent, especially during the first four weeks of classes. It is my intention to introduce them to the practice of looking for God in his creation through critical, biblical thinking and then to write about it with deeper understanding and conviction. What follows is an excerpt from my first day lecture to both chemistry classes. It establishes where I stand with respect to science and the Bible. This is a prelude to what my students can expect from me for the rest of the semester.

If the universe "just happened," if the Logos had not created a cosmos, we would have chaos. In a universe of chaos, there would be no laws of motion, no laws of gravity, no laws of thermodynamics. Math and science would be impossible. I could not stand in front of you today and teach you chemistry because there would be no predictability. John 1:1 says "In the beginning was the word." The Logos, the Word of God, who later in this same chapter of John's Gospel became flesh and dwelt among us, is responsible for everything you can see and touch and feel and hear and sense. Echoing Proverbs 20:12, "The hearing ear, the seeing eye, the Lord has made even both of them," Isaac Newton said, "How came the bodies of animals to be contrived with so much art, and for what ends were their several parts? Was the eye contrived without skill in optics, and the ear without knowledge of sounds? . . . Does it not appear there is a Being incorporeal, living, intelligent?"[19]

The universe displays order and precision. It has been compared to a book, a clock, and a law-governed realm.[20] Many of the early church fathers and natural philosophers during the scientific revolution utilized these metaphors when describing the universe.[21] Psalm 19 reminds us that, as a book, "The heavens declare the Glory of God. . . . Day after day, they pour forth speech" (vv. 1–2 NIV). In a similar vein, the universe exhibits precision, similar to a clock as evidenced by the motions of the stars and planets. A system of laws governs these motions, which are predictable: the sun rises every morning and sets every evening, and so on.

My first challenge of the semester to both cohorts is that they craft a faith integration essay patterned after one I wrote several years ago. "Faith in the Invisible and the Nature of Reality" was published in several online venues. I ask them to summarize what I wrote in their own words, then include their own faith integration

19. As quoted in Meyer, *Return of the God Hypothesis*, 47.
20. Meyer, *Return of the God Hypothesis*, 31.
21. Meyer, *Return of the God Hypothesis*, 33. Meyer includes Anthony the Abbot, Basil the Great, Augustine, Maximus the Confessor, and Thomas Aquinas.

along with a verse from Scripture. The essay deals with our perception of reality. It includes a discussion of both Newton's quotation from *Opticks* and Ps 19. Here is an excerpt:

> As I write, I am looking out my office window at a Tabebuia tree, its pink and yellow trumpet-like flowers in full bloom. They're gorgeous even though the pollen has my eyes itching, and I am sneezing. But what is pink and what is yellow? The colors are caused by photons of light emanating from organic molecules in the flower petals that upon absorbing sunlight reemit that energy as light predominately pink and yellow. (The flowers are colorless in the dark.) The emitted photons are vibrating in the red and yellow portion of the visible electromagnetic spectrum. These wavelengths interact with my retinas to trigger a complex series of chemical reactions that ultimately produce an electrical signal along my optic nerve causing a movie to play in my brain of pink and yellow flowers gently blowing in the breeze. I touch something and even with my eyes closed, I can sense whether it is sharp or smooth, hot or cold, wet or dry, round or square. Receptors in my skin send messages to my brain activating a mental rolodex of stored images. The same case can be made for our sense of smell: Aromatic molecules alight on olfactory receptor neurons in the nose allowing us to distinguish thousands of different odorants.[22]

This essay is eye opening to many of my students who have never contemplated how we sense reality, not to mention how to tie this together with the Bible. The apostle Paul wrote in Romans the "invisible things of him from the creation of the world are clearly seen, being understood by the things that are made, even his eternal power and Godhead" (Rom 1:20). Writing in *On Christian Teaching*, Augustine compared life to a journey and said that we were travelers away from the Lord. "If we wish to return to the homeland, where we can be happy, we must use this world, not enjoy it, in order to discern 'the invisible attributes of God, which are understood through what has been made,' or in other words,

---

22. Rummo, "Faith in the Invisible," paras. 3–5.

to derive eternal and spiritual value from corporeal and temporal things."[23]

One student wrote an excellent essay in response. Here is an excerpt:

> This essay has helped me grasp the concept of our human senses and understand a . . . greater view of reality. The Lord designed the world in such a complex way that everybody should know there has to be a higher power no matter what religion people believe. For example, Ecclesiastes 8:17 says, "Then I saw all that God has done. No one can comprehend what goes on under the sun. Despite all their efforts to search it out, no one can discover its meaning. Even if the wise claim they know, they cannot comprehend it."

Five students chose to write about another question I posited in class: the creation of dark matter, as discussed in an article from *Annalen der Physik*, "Is Matter Still Being Created in the Universe?"[24] This was no easy task and several students wrestled with the concept of dark matter and whether it was only created in the early universe or is it still filling the universe today, and what does this have to do with Scripture?

There is far more about the universe that we don't understand than what we do understand. Writing in *Amazing Truths, How Science and the Bible Agree*, Dr. Michael Guillen explains that astronomers have concluded that "dark energy comprises some sixty-eight percent of the total universe and dark matter about twenty-seven percent. That means only five percent of the entire universe is visible to us. That astonishing revelation bears emphasizing. Everything we call scientific knowledge is based on a pittance of what there is to know about our world. *Ninety-five percent of it is hidden from us.*"[25]

Four students wrote that they believe matter is still being created in the universe and made reference to the creation account

---

23. Augustine, *On Christian Teaching*, 10.
24. Bergström, "Dark Matter Evidence."
25. Guillen, *Amazing Truths*, 60.

in Genesis, quoting Gen 1:1. One student took this a step further and wrote,

> Genesis 1:2 says that the earth "was without form and void and darkness was over the face of the earth." This verse confirms that the earth itself (matter) was created from nothing. But is matter still being created? Hebrews 11:3 states, "By faith we understand that the universe was created by the word of God, so that what is seen was not made out of things visible." The Bible's description of matter is very interesting as it explains that instances of matter being created can be attributed to the magnitude of God's power.

One student pushed back and made the case for matter not being created in the universe, and wrote, "Einstein said that matter could neither be created nor destroyed. It can only go through physical and chemical changes but it is the same matter before and after. Ecclesiastes 1:9 says, 'History merely repeats itself. It has all been done before. Nothing under the sun is truly new.'"

In the next section, I will showcase examples of faith integration essays from students in my pre-nursing cohort. I have listed the articles that were available to them along with the number of students who chose to write about each topic. I have included a short synopsis for each article to orient the reader and give a sense of what the students were reading and responding to in their essays.

FAITH INTEGRATION IN THE SOCIAL SCIENCES FOR THE PRE-NURSING COHORT

Listed below in table 4 are some of the current article selections for the pre-nursing cohort. Topics are almost all related to the health-sciences.[26]

---

26. These are listed by author in the bibliography. All of these articles were published in the *Wall Street Journal*.

Table 4 Faith Integration Essay Topics for Pre-Nursing Cohort

Title of Article	Student Essays
Rachel Feintzeig, "Stressed Nurses Wonder: How to Quit a Job When It's Your Calling?" Jan. 10, 2022	40
Elizabeth Bernstein, "How to Deal with Stress in Your Life: Embrace It," Aug. 28, 2021	
Andrea Petersen, "A Rise in Suicides by Young Children Leaves Families Searching for Answers," June 5, 2022	13
Jenny Taitz, "Honest Communication in the Age of Ghosting," Aug. 27, 2021	12
Richard McNally, "'The Good Life' Review: The Habit of Happiness," Jan. 11, 2023	8
Saeed Shah, "As Hunger Spreads in Afghanistan, Hospitals Fill with Premature, Dying Babies," Jan. 28, 2022	6
Ryan Burge, "There's No Crisis of Faith on Campus," Feb. 24, 2022	6
Betsy Morris, "How Old Do You Feel? The Answer Can Reveal a Lot about Your Health, Scientists Say," Dec. 5, 2022	6
Kate Murphy, "The Covid Fear Isn't Going Anywhere for a While," Aug. 15, 2021	5
Gloria Mark, "How to Restore Our Dwindling Attention Span," Jan. 6, 2023	5
David DeSteno, "Is Religion Good for Your Health?" June 8, 2023	3
Lisa Bannon, "When AI Overrules the Nurses Caring for You," June 15, 2023	2

STUDENTS AND STRESS

It is no surprise that over several semesters, the two articles dealing with stress generated the most interest among my students. Rachel Feintzeig's article about stressed nurses and Elizabeth Bernstein's article on embracing stress approached the issue from two different sides. Feintzeig wrote of the stress and burnout nurses are facing as a result of the COVID-19 pandemic. A 2021 survey of 6,568 nurses revealed that two-thirds of them were considering leaving their careers. Bernstein's article dealt more with coping with stress through application of what psychologists recommend is "an ability to see reality clearly and embrace all our emotions, both pleasant and unpleasant . . . through a widely used and standard therapeutic approach called Acceptance and Commitment Therapy (ACT)."[27]

The following are selected, unedited excerpts from student essays on the topic of stress. Each paragraph is from a different student. I have added a short summary at the end of their comments.

"God is in control. He has a plan for every one of us and I always try and remind myself of that. Sometimes it's easy to think we're very unimportant and we're not good enough, but in God's eyes, we are so loved and important."

"As a support for a Scripture from the Bible, consider Proverbs 12:25, 'Anxiety in a man's heart weighs him down but a good word makes him glad.'"

"This article started to bring emotions to me, because a lot of family issues have come about during this first year. Because of these family issues, it's been hard to keep up with everything, especially nursing classes. . . . I am going to put some of these stress relieving steps into my life . . . the first step [is to] slow yourself down. Matthew 6:34 says 'Therefore do not worry about tomorrow, for tomorrow will worry about itself. Each day has enough trouble of its own.'"

"Sometimes being stressed makes me even more stressed. I believe this article was a gift and an eye-opener to me, and now I learned that when stress is present, I will accept, strategize, and hopefully overcome it."

"One of the pieces of advice in the article was to create a mantra. . . . Committing to memorizing scripture is one of the best decisions I've made especially for times when I am feeling overwhelmed."

"Because my faith relationship with God [is] such a big part of my life, reading the Bible is a big part of calming down and resetting my mind so I can get back up and continue with school or work. A verse that has stuck with me is James 1:2–3. It says

---

27. Bernstein, "How to Deal with Stress," para. 6.

'Consider it all joy my brothers when you meet trials of various kinds. For you know the testing of your faith produces steadfastness.' This reminds me that God gives me hardships for a reason."

"No matter the circumstances, each of us will face stress and therefore it is important that we learn how to embrace it and live with it. . . . Psalm 55:22 states, 'Cast your burden on the Lord, and he will sustain you; he will never permit the righteous to be moved.' By giving our stress over to the Lord, we are able to give it to the only one who can handle the problems caused by stress."

"When I am stressed, having anxiety, scared, etc. [Psalm 23] is the scripture I quote the most. The psalm uses a metaphor of a shepherd's care for his sheep to describe the wisdom, strength and kindness of our God."

"Every time I read Psalm 46:10, the verse up over my TV, 'Be still and know that I am God,' I think about my 'stressful' fast paced life that really has the same number of seconds in it as everyone else and as every great person and hero in the Bible."

"This article made me think a bit about why I want to become a nurse. It made me reflect how I believe that nursing is my calling. I cannot wait to see how God uses my calling for his glory. In 1 Peter 4:10 it says, 'Each of you should use whatever gifts you have received to serve others, as faithful stewards of God's grace in various forms.'"

I was happy to read that my students appreciated these two articles and said they learned something from reading them. I was also happy to read that they are dealing with the stress of college despite personal problems and stressful family situations.

The APA reported, "The potential long-term consequences of the persistent stress and trauma created by the pandemic are particularly serious for our country's youngest individuals, known as Generation Z (Gen Z). Our 2020 survey shows that Gen Z teens (ages 13–17) and Gen Z adults (ages 18–23) are facing unprecedented uncertainty, are experiencing elevated stress and are already reporting symptoms of depression."[28] Despite these bleak statistics, many of my students reaffirmed that nursing is a calling

---

28. American, "Stress in America," 1.

from God, others have learned to use Scriptures effectively, memorizing selected Bible verses as mantras to help alleviate stress. Almost all of the essays demonstrated a desire to trust the Lord more, allowing him to help manage stressful situations.

STUDENTS ON YOUTH SUICIDE

"Before 10-year-old Kelly Wright killed herself, there was no warning, says her father, Stuart Wright. The bubbly child who loved to draw, hike and go canoeing was showing her parents dance moves the night before she died, Mr. Wright says."[29] So begins this tragic article about the rise in suicides among young people. The number of youth suicides has risen dramatically in recent years, quadrupling among females between the ages of 10 to 14. Among males the same age, the rate tripled.[30] This article was the second-most popular among my students. Selected excerpts from their essays appear below. I have added a short summary at the end of their comments.

"I believe if we rely on the world to give us happiness, we will be let down time and time again. Matthew 11:28 says, 'Come to me, all you who are weary and burdened and I will give you rest.' This verse points to God as a solution. . . . Therapy is encouraged for those who are struggling mentally, however, incorporating God into our lives will be the most powerful change. No child can feel poorly about themselves if they know how special they were for Jesus Christ to die for them."

"With my background in psychology, I am very passionate about being a mental health advocate. . . . I also have struggles with my mental health. . . . I have also lost my best friend to suicide a few years ago so this topic is something I am passionate about."

---

29. Petersen, "Rise in Suicides," para. 1.

30. Among females, ages 10 to 14, the rate of suicide more than tripled between 2007 and 2020 from 0.5 per 100,000 to 2.0 per 100,000 according to data from the National Center for Health Statistics. Among males the same age, the rate jumped from 1.2 per 100,000 to 3.6 per 100,000 over the same period. Petersen, "Rise in Suicides," para. 4.

"This article impacted me a lot, and now, I am wondering how children of nine and ten years old can think about suicide. When I was that age all I thought about was playing. It is the Lord who 'gives life and takes it away; He leads us to the grave and rescues us from it,' 1 Samuel 2:6."

"I grew up in a school district and neighborhood that would unite to celebrate the life lost of a different daughter, son, sibling or friend almost annually. I along with my sister and dad struggle with severe depression and anxiety; mental health checks and conversations [became] a priority in our household and I believe these were pivotal moments in working towards healing for each of us as individuals and as a family. God encourages us to call upon him in our darkest valleys. Psalm 55:22 reads, 'Give your burdens to the Lord and he will take care of you. He will not let the godly slip and fall.'"

"I was fifteen years old and blinded by my [then] current and insignificant problems. I could not see outside of my narrow-minded thoughts and felt as if the world was crashing down around me. It came to a point where I sat on my bathroom floor and debated taking an entire bottle of sleeping pills, hoping it would be painless. However, my mom had open conversations about suicide with me from a younger age and I knew it would not be worth the pain that I would cause everyone around me. Jeremiah 29:11 says, 'For I know the plans I have for you, declares the Lord. Plans to prosper you and no to harm you, plans to give you hope and a future.'"

"This article was very informative and has given me a different view of children. One Bible verse I would share with someone dealing with suicidal thoughts is, 'Do you not know that you are God's temple and that God's spirit dwells in you?' This demonstrates how important every single person is and that God is with us no matter what."

In chapter 2 I wrote that Gen Z has fewer inhibitions about discussing their mental health openly. The number of essays (eleven) and the intimate details of my students' lives they were willing to reveal in their responses confirms this. In one sense, I find it unbelievable. College was the best four years of my life. I was independent, happy, and focused on my coursework. In contrast, during my five years of teaching at PBA, four students have admitted to me that they had considered taking their own lives.[31] The cause in almost every case was depression or anxiety from some trauma, real or perceived. Several have told me, matter-of-factly, that they are seeing a therapist. Gen Z is more likely to self-harm, have a poorer body image, skip sleep, be overweight, and have depression.[32] But, as mental health challenges have risen, the stigma about mental health has decreased due, primarily, to normalized mental health treatment, social media which has destigmatized mental health disorders, and an overall general increase in what we know about the causes and therapies.[33] I am glad my students are so willing to discuss openly their mental health challenges. Their transparency and vulnerability allow me to be a better-informed mentor to them.

STUDENTS AND GHOSTING

"Ghosting" occurs when communication from someone we know suddenly stops for no apparent reason. "When someone we know morphs from attentive to aloof without explanation, it's disconcerting and maddening."[34] There is even such a thing as Christian ghosting.[35] It's easy to ghost people on social media, to cut them off from chat groups and friend circles. Given the amount of time students spend on their phones looking at social media, many have been hurt when a friend ghosted them.

---

31. By this I mean before coming to PBA and not recently, i.e., the week or month prior to our conversation. Faculty are required by law to notify the proper authorities about any student who shares suicidal thoughts.
32. Matthews-King, "Generation Z Teenagers."
33. Cuncic, "Why Gen Z Is More Open."
34. Taitz, "Honest Communication," para. 4.
35. Corey, "Christian Ghosting."

There is a right way and a wrong way to break off communications with a friend.[36] Cutting them off suddenly shows a lack of love, it destroys relationships, and it almost always negates the possibility for restoration. The Bible tells us to "love our neighbors as ourselves" (Mark 12:31). To disappear from a friend's life without an explanation is hurtful, especially if it is a boyfriend or a girlfriend, so I was not surprised to see this article was in a close tie for the second most-popular faith integration. The following are selected, unedited excerpts from student essays on the topic.

"I have learned over the years that having that difficult conversation benefits me and the other person greatly. Ephesians 4:29 says, 'Do not let any unwholesome talk come out of your mouths, but only what is helpful for building others up according to their needs, that it may benefit those who listen.'"

"Ghosting puts the interest of self and comfort over the interests of the other individual or individuals. As Christians especially, we are to treat others with a level of respect that places a concern for them above a concern for ourselves in the hopes that they too will be considering us in that way."

"The Bible says in Matthew 18:15, 'If your brother sins against you, go and tell him his fault, between you and him alone. If he listens to you, you have gained your brother.' God wants us to confront problems head on. There is much comfort and healing in communication. Friendships and relationships will be better protected if there is communication instead of silence."

"Ghosting and rejecting people is not how we show kindness to each other. We should always be courteous and kind and even if you are rejected by others, you aren't rejected by God. It even says in the Bible in Psalms 94:14, 'For the Lord will not reject his people; he will never forsake his inheritance.' God's people include anyone who believes in him and they, henceforth, become his inheritance. Translation: God will never ghost you."

---

36. I should make the distinction between a friend and an unhealthy association with a person that has threatened or carried out abuse or violence. In such cases, ghosting is wholly appropriate.

STUDENTS ON THE QUESTION OF THE CRISIS OF FAITH ON CAMPUS

The findings of a recent survey of college students by sociologists Damon Mayrl of Colby College and Jeremy Euker of Baylor University was the subject of this article, written by the well-known church leader, podcaster, and Baptist pastor Ryan Burge, who is also a professor of political science at Eastern Illinois University. The study concluded that what influenced students the most about their religious beliefs were not necessarily the professors and what was being taught in the classroom, but the "social context that young people find themselves in when they go to college.... The student's ideological beliefs started moving closer to those of their roommates."[37] The Bible has much to say about the importance of choosing the right friends. First Corinthians 15:53 plainly states, "Do not be deceived: 'Bad company ruins good morals.'" I was curious to see what my students would say about this article, especially in light of the recent spontaneous revival that occurred last year at Asbury College in Lexington, Kentucky. The following are selected excerpts.

"This article made me hopeful and happy. I am glad that students in college are remaining firm in their faith. As a nursing student, it is so important to remain strong in faith."

"Although I am a freshman, I have found that I have leaned into my faith more than ever before. Being at a Christian university has deeply influenced my faith. Having the ability to be in classrooms with Christian professors, Christian peers and community that genuinely cares about the well-being of its students has been the greatest blessing to me. James 1:2–3 says 'Consider it pure joy, my brothers and sisters, whenever you face trials of many kinds because you know the testing of your faith produces perseverance.' Trials can teach us new things about God, about ourselves and the world that God has created around us."

"Fortunately, close friends of mine who are in similar stages in the walk of faith are going to be in my cohort and continue to

---

37. Burge, "'There's No Crisis," para. 9.

encourage and build me up in faith. I am reminded of 2 Timothy 4:7, 'I have fought the good fight, I have finished the race, I have kept the faith.'"

STUDENTS ON DYING, PREMATURE AFGHANI BABIES

When the United States withdrew the remainder of its troops from Afghanistan during the summer of 2021, it created a power vacuum that the Taliban quickly filled. In violation of its agreement with the United States, it seized control of the government. Economic sanctions from the West quickly followed, producing an economic collapse that caused widespread starvation. It was reported that half of the population faced acute hunger and "one million children [were] in danger of dying from malnutrition."[38] I was interested to see how many of my students would be moved by this article and choose it as one of their faith integration assignments. It resonated with six students, among them several who would like to work in neonatal care units. The following excerpts showcase their comments.

"As Christians, we are called to give and to tend to the poor because that is exactly what Jesus did."

"After reading this article and the families' stories, I want to go to Afghanistan and feed these families and provide them with what they need."

"Reading this article broke my heart. While getting closer to the end I was hoping that there would be a positive aspect or hope for the whole situation but there was not."

"This article really speaks to me because I want to be a NICU nurse. Before reading this article, I already knew that premature babies have a hard chance fighting for survival. Now, it makes me even more sad knowing that in poverty, premature babies have almost little to no chance of survival. I want to dedicate my life to helping others. I do not want to sit back and watch people die.

---

38. Shah, "As Hunger Spreads in Afghanistan," para. 4.

I want to be the type of person who will try everything I possibly can to save a life. 'I can do all things through him who strengthens me'" (Phil 4:13).

"The people interviewed in this article say over and over that they just wish someone would help. Luke 6:30 commands us to 'Give everyone who asks you and if anyone takes what belongs to you, do not demand it back.'"

The article does, in fact, close on a depressing note. A man takes his three-year-old daughter, Laila, to a square in central Kabul "to sell her to a passerby" for $200 or $300. "Anyone with that sort of money would be able to look after her better than he could. He didn't find anyone to pay."[39]

STUDENTS ON DEVELOPING A HABIT OF HAPPINESS

Richard J. McNally's article about developing a habit of happiness was the subject that five students chose to write about. It was the sixth most popular article on the list, and reading their responses and biblical integrations was a delightful diversion from the previous articles that dealt with serious social concerns and mental-health-related disorders. McNally answers the question, "What constitutes a life well-lived?" by summarizing the "Longest Scientific Study of Happiness."[40] The authors, psychiatrist Robert Waldinger and clinical psychologist Marc Schulz, followed the lives of hundreds of people across the twentieth and twenty-first centuries, and concluded what was most important to happiness was "the importance of positive interpersonal relationships throughout the lifespan."[41] Another aspect of social fitness discovered in the study was what the authors termed "cognitive flexibility, exemplified by the capacity to see the world through another person's eyes, to express empathetic understanding, and to attend

---

39. Shah, "As Hunger Spreads in Afghanistan," para. 29.
40. McNally, "'Good Life' Review."
41. McNally, "'Good Life' Review," para. 2.

fully to others."[42] My nursing students agreed unanimously with the study's findings. Excerpts from their essays follow.

"Psalm 126:5 says, 'Those who sow in tears shall reap in joy.' Being God's children doesn't mean that our sadness or our fears go away, it means that we have someone stronger than either of those combined, backing us up and supporting us in our journey through life."

"The article reminded me that God designed us to be in relationship/fellowship with others. The connections we form with others often allows us to experience God's love through encouragement. John Stuart Mill (1806–1873) wrote, 'Those only are happy who have their minds fixed on some object other than their own happiness, on the happiness of others.' This is in keeping with Philippians 2:2–4, '. . . in humility, value others above yourself, not looking to your own interests but each of you to the interests of the others.'"

STUDENTS ON THE PERSISTENCE OF COVID FEARS

The article, "The Covid Fear Isn't Going Anywhere for a While," no longer appears on the list since COVID-19 is now a memory, and a bad one at that. Nonetheless, five students chose to write about this article during the fall 2022 semester. The author suggested a three-step approach to dealing with COVID-bred fear: become aware of the fear and acknowledge it, learn how to slow down and reflect on the self, and face the fear, taking control of it, because "Covid fear isn't going anywhere for a while."[43]

The students who wrote about this article all agreed that fear and anxiety in general must be embraced and not ignored. One student added a fourth suggestion, "to give fear and anxiety over to God and trust him."

Each of the students integrated Scriptures that directly speak about stress and anxiety. One student wrote about 1 Pet

---

42. McNally, "'Good Life' Review," para. 7.
43. Murphy, "Covid Fear."

5:7, "Cast all your anxiety on him because he cares for you." Another wrote about 2 Tim 1:7, "For God did not give us a spirit of fear. He gave us a spirit of power and love and a good mind." A third student included Phil 4:6–7, "Be anxious for nothing but in everything, by prayer and supplication, with thanksgiving, let your requests be made known to God, and the peace of God, which surpasses all understanding will guard your hearts and minds through Christ Jesus."

The students who wrote these essays were in high school during the height of COVID lockdowns and had to endure their junior and senior years attending class from home, sitting in front of a computer screen. Some were denied their senior class trips, senior proms, and graduation ceremonies. But the lessons learned by these nursing students will be helpful in the years ahead as they help their patients deal with their own fears and anxieties.

STUDENTS ON GETTING OLD

I was surprised that any of my teenage, Gen Z students would be interested in reading an article about getting old, although on occasion I have an "adult"[44] in this class (and sure enough, she was one of the students among the four who chose this topic to write about). The secret to avoiding getting old is to think and to feel young. In the article, the author distinguishes between "subjective age" or "psychological age" and chronological age, citing studies by psychologists and gerontologists who claim "there might be ways to improve physical health by making yourself feel younger—or at least taking a positive attitude toward aging."[45] I was all ears about this article from a selfish point of view and therefore extremely interested to read what my four students had to say.

"Feeling negative about one's own age generates more stress in one's life and stimulates cortisol production and c-reactive

---

44. Technically speaking, they are all adults. Anyone over the age of eighteen is considered an adult. But I have had students in my classes in their late twenties who decided to go back to school and earn a nursing degree.

45. Morris, "How Old Do You Feel?," para. 2.

protein which can lead to health issues. Studies by the Yale School of Public Health suggest that our life experiences and environment we grew up in often influence our perceptions of aging. These biases are not hard to overcome, however. This is biblical. Proverbs 17:22 states, 'A merry heart doeth good like medicine but a broken spirit dries the bones.'"

"While taking care of my siblings while my parents were busy, I could see my parents' stress and their age starting to show. If my parents had known 2 Corinthians 4:16, 'Therefore we do not lose heart, though outwardly we are wasting away yet inwardly we are being renewed day by day,' they would have been more at ease with the idea of aging."

The article and this student's response in particular reminded me of the verse, "As a man thinks in his heart, so is he" (Prov 23:7). Scripture reminds us to guard our heart, for out of it "flow the springs of life" (Prov 4:23). I have always thought it important to think young and honor God's temple by taking care of it, including eating mindfully, exercising often, and avoiding harmful substances.

SEVENTIES SOFT ROCK AND X POSTS[46] TO POINT STUDENTS TO CHRIST

It's not just in the academic rigor of writing faith integration essays that students can find God, but also in the more common, everyday experiences such as a song they might hear or something they see on social media that sparks their curiosity. With all the negative attention social media receives, I thought it would be a good idea to highlight a positive aspect of it. In this section, I will briefly describe two unconventional methods I use to point students to Christ.

The first is to play a variety of seventies soft-rock songs each semester before the start of class. What began as something I did simply for myself to help me relax while the students filed in, never did I realize how impactful this was to my students until taking a

---

46. When Elon Musk purchased Twitter, he changed the name to X. Tweets are no longer called "tweets" but "posts."

group of them on a mission trip during the summer of 2023. We had landed in Lima, Peru, and were waiting in line at immigration. I had been the last one in line. When I finally emerged on the other side of the security doors, one of my students ran up to me and said excitedly, "Professor Rummo, listen!" The music being played in one of the airport shops was "Another Day in Paradise," by Phil Collins. "I remember when you played this song for us and explained what it was about," she said. "This was the best part of your chemistry class!" I'm not sure if playing seventies soft-rock songs should be "the best part of my chemistry class," so I was stunned that this student recognized the song and remembered what I had said about its message. For the uninitiated, see the lyrics online.

When I played this for my class earlier that semester, I explained the Old Testament concept of *hesed*, the Hebrew word for "help or unfailing kindness to the helpless."[47] It is exemplified by God's people in many places in the Old Testament—Elijah and Elisha for example (1 Kgs 17:7–16; 2 Kgs 4: 1–7)—and in countless instances by Jesus in the New Testament. It is what gripped the heart of the singer-songwriter Phil Collins who wrote "Another Day in Paradise" to highlight the plight of the homeless. Collins was criticized because of his wealth, which his critics thought disqualified him to write about the homeless. But Collins shot back, "When I drive down the street, I see the same things everyone else sees. It's a misconception that if you have a lot of money you're somehow out of touch with reality."[48] What follows in table 5 is a short list of some of the other songs, with a short, one- or two-sentence description of how they might prompt reflections on faith, God, etc.[49]

---

47. Waltke, *Old Testament Theology*, 850, 853.
48. Collins, "Another Day in Paradise," para. 12.
49. One might ask, What makes a song Christian? "Something is Christian if it reflects the theological convictions of the Christian community in its content, purpose, message and life implications; all of these rest on theologically informed criteria." Estep et al., *Theology for Christian Education*, 26. Almost none of these songs are Christian by that definition. They are conversation starters, which sometimes lead to deeper theological considerations.

Table 5 Selected Seventies Soft-Rock Songs

"Turn, Turn, Turn," The Byrds	The words are taken directly from Eccl 3, "To everything there is a purpose..."
"Fire and Rain," James Taylor	Life has its ups and downs. James Taylor recognized this, imploring Jesus for help in the second verse.
"Disappear," Hoobastank	Disappear, "explores themes of loneliness, isolation, and the desire to escape from the pressures of life."[50] The listener is left with the haunting question about the identity of the person that draws near to us when all the others are nowhere to be seen.
"Kiss from a Rose," Seal	The power of love. Seal associated the image of a rose with the red color of a Bloody Mary and "compared the feeling of being consumed by love to being drunk."[51] "Be not drunk with wine..." (Eph 5:18 KJV)
"Dust in the Wind," Kansas	During a dark time in his life, Kerry Livgren, lead singer of Kansas, wrote that mankind is windblown dust. He later became a Christian.
"Woodstock," Crosby, Stills, and Nash	The song is an allusion to Eden. We know the world is not quite right. Inside we all long to be where we were created to be. One day all will be restored.
"100 Years," Five for Fighting	The stages of life: the teens, the prime of life as a young married couple, kids come along, a mid-life crisis, maturity, and finally, old age. Cherish every stage.

This was just another creative way to remind my students, "One must learn to remember, to attend, to come awake, remain receptive, or run the risk of missing God who is everywhere incognito."[52]

SOCIAL MEDIA X POSTS POINT TO CHRIST

I am known on campus by some of my students as the "Paparazzi Professor." I am always photographing students in laboratory

---

50. Pitts, "Meaning Behind: Disappear," para. 1.
51. Duncan, "Meaning Behind: Kiss from a Rose," para. 7.
52. Brown, *Life Observed*, 34.

classes and sharing them on Facebook. Several of these have been published in magazines such as *Chemical & Engineering News*[53] and *Good News Florida*.[54] During the spring and fall 2023 semesters, I invited students to follow me on X. I offered students one point of extra credit, up to a maximum of five, applicable to each of the three in-class exams, for every post they engaged with. An engagement included a "like," a "repost," and a one-to-two paragraph summary of the linked article that also had to include at least one reference from Scripture. Table 6 lists nine of the dozens of topics I posted.

Table 6 Selected X Topics Posted

Missionaries You Should Know	A short bio of Adoniram Judson
Sinners in the Hands of an Angry Goddess	A review of Apple's new iPhone ad appeasing Mother Nature
How Did the Human Mind Come to Be?	A post by the Discovery Institute
The Chemistry of Pumpkins	A post from the American Chemical Society (ACS)
Incredible Design of Human Muscles	A post by the Discovery Institute
How to Live Unashamed of the Gospel	A post from The Gospel Coalition (TGC)
Is It OK for a Christian to Cuss?	A post from Belief.net
Nobel Chemistry Winner Who Failed	Moungi Bawendi failed his first college chemistry exam
Seeing Is Believing	A post by Dr. Michael Guillen who turns this on its head and shows that believing is seeing

The responses from the students were overwhelming. I counted well over one hundred interactions. About half the class in each semester took part in this experiment. The point of the X exercise was twofold: to help them realize that God is everywhere

---

53. Howes, "Scenes from Where Chemists Work." Bettenhausen, "Chemistry in Pictures."

54. Rummo, "Educating the Whole Person."

even if he is "incognito," and that social media does have redeeming qualities if it is used for good purposes.

SUMMARY

In this chapter I highlighted the methods I use in the classroom to fulfill the first part of PBA's motto to "enlighten minds" in reaching Gen Z. By teaching students how to organically integrate faith into the coursework, they learn how to recognize God is everywhere present. Over the course of the last three years, I have collected over one hundred of these essays[55] written by students in response to articles from secular sources that dealt with relevant topics in the pure sciences and health-related issues impacting society. The excerpts I shared in this chapter speak for themselves. They are powerful testimonies that demonstrate an ability to integrate Scripture into many life situations.[56] My students' essays revealed a personal hunger for the gospel. Many in the nursing cohort wrote that they were inspired and encouraged by the articles they read. Some were saddened. They all wrote that they had learned valuable lessons that would help them in their future careers in nursing. While most of my students are well-adjusted and happy, some admitted to struggles with anxiety and depression. A few said they were seeing a therapist and were committed to overcome their challenges. As I mentioned earlier, it's not only in the academic rigor of the classroom that students can find God, but also in the more common, everyday experiences of life. This was the method behind the madness of sharing with them the music I remembered as a college student, and still enjoy to this day, as

---

55. The essays in this chapter are counted separately from the essays written about "A Sisterhood of Nurses" that appear in chapter 2, "Know Their Stories." I have collected over two hundred essays from both cohorts in the last three academic years as a part of my research.

56. Keller, *Center Church*, 89. Keller calls this "intentional contextualization," which he defines as "giving people *the Bible's answers*, which they may not at all want to hear, *to questions about life* that people in their particular time and place are asking, *in language and forms* they can comprehend, and *through appeals and arguments* with force they can feel, even if they reject them."

well as social media to help them see that God is everywhere. As the songwriter Maltbie D. Babcock (1858 1901) wrote, "This is my father's world."[57]

In the next chapter I will share several examples of faith integrations from the chemistry laboratory. Jesus often used illustrations to teach his disciples spiritual truths. Like "Show and Tell," they have the ability to make a lasting impact.

---

57. Babcock, "This Is My Father's World," stanza 1. "This is my Father's world,/And to my listening ears/All nature sings, and round me rings/The music of the spheres."

CHAPTER FIVE

Integrating Faith in the Chemistry Laboratory

After the knowledge of, and obedience to, the will of God, the next aim must be to know something of his attributes of wisdom, power and goodness as evidenced by His handiwork.

—JAMES JOULE (1818–1889)[1]

INTRODUCTION

JESUS USED VISUALS FREQUENTLY when teaching his disciples. A farmer sowing seeds scatters them on different types of soil, a shepherd with one hundred sheep loses one, a man buys a field and finds buried treasure—these are just three of the many visuals Jesus used to convey important, eternal truths. Visuals are a powerful means to convey truths. They have the power to evoke emotions and captivate audiences within seconds.[2] The chemistry labora-

---

1. Blattman, "James Joule," para. 7.
2. Ucha, "Impact of Visual Content."

tory is a platform for visual learning. It allows students to visualize theoretical concepts that they learn in lecture or from reading in their textbooks. Visuals often facilitate a more memorable learning experience than either the spoken or the written word. I can explain the chemistry of rocket propulsion. I can show my students a video of a space shuttle launch. But when I drop a glowing wooden splint into a test tube of molten potassium chlorate and a flame shoots out with a loud *whoosh!* followed by a plume of acrid smoke, that gets their attention. In this chapter I will explain how I use the experiments in my two laboratory classes as a platform for faith integration through the powerful medium of visuals. Some faith integrations also include a component of social responsibility. Examples of both are included.

"THE LAWS OF NATURE ARE WRITTEN BY THE HAND OF GOD IN THE LANGUAGE OF MATHEMATICS."[3]

When students enter the laboratory, I want them to remember that God is in a very real sense their lab partner. As a Christian teaching at a Christian college, I have the responsibility to create an awareness that God is the creator of all things, and that this truth applies in the reality of the laboratory as well as in the theory of the classroom. Colossians 1:16–17 says, "For by him all things were created, in heaven and on earth, visible and invisible, whether thrones or dominions or rulers or authorities—all things were created through him and for him. And he is before all things, and in him all things hold together." Isaac Newton's statement, "All my discoveries have been made in answer to prayer,"[4] is not some token mental ascension to nature. Newton realized that one of the roles of the Holy Spirit was to illuminate his understanding, not just to spiritual truths, but to all truth. Similarly, Louis Pasteur (1822–1895) realized this when he said, "Science brings men

---

3. Attributed to Galileo Galilei.
4. Blattman, "Quotes on God," para. 6.

nearer to God."[5] The converse could also be said, God brings men nearer to science.

James Clerk Maxwell (1831–1879) was a physicist who specialized in the study of electromagnetic radiation. From his work in the laboratory flowed the four famous equations that led to the technological revolution of the nineteenth and twentieth centuries. Maxwell understood how faith in the God of creation was a necessary component for the understanding of all natural phenomena. This was Maxwell's prayer:

> Almighty God, who has created man in Thine own image, and made him a living soul that he might seek after Thee, and have dominion over Thy creatures, teach us to study the works of Thy hands, that we may subdue the earth to our use, and strengthen the reason for Thy service; so to receive Thy blessed Word, that we may believe on him whom Thou has sent, to give us the knowledge of salvation and the remission of sins. All of which we ask in the name of the same Jesus Christ, our Lord.[6]

In my laboratory classes, I have many opportunities to demonstrate the intersection of pure, empirical science with philosophy, metaphysics, and biblical theology by utilizing the powerful medium of visuals. God created us as holistic beings with body, mind, soul, and spirit. We were not destined to live compartmentalized lives or to partition our thinking into artificially created "magisteria."[7] What follows are actual examples from several laboratory classes I regularly teach.

---

5. Lamont, "Louis Pasteur (1822–1895)," para. 28.
6. Lamont, "Great Creation Scientists," para. 27.
7. "Magisteria" are the invention of Stephen Jay Gould (1941–2002), "a secular Jew who did not believe in God." He regarded religion and science as separate forms of knowledge. C. S. Lewis called this "scientism," or the belief that only science can offer the correct explanations for natural phenomena. Shermer, "Meaning of Life," 83.

CHEMICAL CHANGE OR PHYSICAL CHANGE? JUDGE NOT BY APPEARANCES

During one laboratory procedure, students mix solutions of different chemical compounds to determine whether a chemical reaction has occurred. Indications of a chemical reaction include a color change, the formation of a precipitate, the evolution of heat or light, or the appearance of bubbles indicating that a gas has formed. Based on observations alone, the students are to judge whether a chemical reaction has occurred. At the end of the lab, I bring out a large Florence flask that contains a clear, colorless liquid. With one tap of a spatula over the opening of the flask, the solution quickly turns into a white, opaque solid and the flask becomes too hot to handle comfortably. I ask: "What just happened? Was it chemistry or something else?"

Almost without exception, students judge it to have been a chemical change. But what has happened is that a tiny, almost invisible crystal of sodium acetate that was on the tip of the spatula was introduced on to the surface of what is an unstable, aqueous, supersaturated solution of the same compound. The crystal provides the template for the molecules to align themselves into a more stable crystalline state and the entire flask solidifies in a matter of seconds.

To the student's surprise, this is not a chemical change but a physical change, despite three of the five criteria having been met. This demo provides a perfect segue into the Bible's teachings about making judgments based on insufficient evidence. The verse we discuss, "Judge not according to appearance, but judge righteous judgment" (John 7:24), is an excellent reminder that in both science and human relations, judging only by appearances often results in erroneous conclusions.

ATOMIC THEORY AND THE CROSS OF CHRIST

Demonstrating atomic theory in the laboratory is done by passing an electric current through a sample of hydrogen gas in a glass tube.

The hydrogen glows and the light it emits, when viewed through a spectroscope, reveals the nature of the energy levels of the electron in the atom's orbitals. Although the model for the atom we derive from this simple experiment is incorrect, we still teach it because it does explain the wavelengths of the emission spectrum of hydrogen. This experiment celebrates our earliest attempts to understand atomic theory, when in Europe, at the turn of the twentieth century, great advances were being made towards that end.

In 1904 the British physicist and Nobel laureate Sir Joseph John Thomson (1856–1940), who had discovered the electron, proposed his "Plum Pudding Model" of the atom, characterizing it as a smear of positive and negative charges much like pudding with embedded raisins (which the British called *plums*).

Five years later, Hans Geiger (1882–1945) and Ernest Marsden (1889–1970), working under the direction of Ernest Rutherford (1871–1937) at Manchester University, devised an experiment to further elucidate atomic structure by bombarding a thin sheet of gold foil with a stream of alpha particles. Instead of the alpha particles passing straight through, some were deflected at various angles and a few ricocheted back at 180 degrees.

This was a stunning finding. It took several more years for Rutherford to explain the observed phenomenon, which he did in a lecture he gave at Cambridge University:

> It was quite the most incredible event that has ever happened to me in my life. It was almost as incredible as if you fired a 15-inch shell at a piece of tissue paper and it came back and hit you. On consideration, I realized that this scattering backward must be the result of a single collision, and when I made calculations I saw that it was impossible to get anything of that order of magnitude unless you took a system in which the greater part of the mass of the atom was concentrated in a minute nucleus. It was then that I had the idea of an atom with a minute massive centre, carrying a charge.[8]

---

8. Rutherford and Ratcliffe, "Forty Years of Physics," 68–69.

INTEGRATING FAITH IN THE CHEMISTRY LABORATORY

In 1913, Danish physicist Niels Bohr (1885–1962) presented a complete picture of the atom, what we call a planetary model, with negatively charged electrons orbiting a positively charged nucleus. He had used a combination of classical physics with the new concept of *quantization* proposed by German physicist Max Planck. Here is the mathematical expression that describes the Bohr equation for the one-electron hydrogen atom:

$$r = \frac{n^2 h^2}{4\pi^2 k e^2 m}$$

The beauty of this equation is its simplicity: n is an integer—1, 2, 3, etc.—and corresponds to the principal energy levels of the atom. All the other symbols are either numbers or constants that were known at the time. When this expression is solved, we obtain a picture of the hydrogen atom, its lone electron orbiting a single proton in a circular path with a radius of 0.53 Å in the ground state. Despite several flawed assumptions, Bohr's model accurately explained observed phenomena such as the visible emission spectrum of hydrogen. It is why we still teach this laboratory procedure today.

That a rudimentary model of the atom could be elucidated by simply observing (and measuring) the wavelengths of the four lines generated by the emission spectrum of hydrogen always fascinates students. But even though Niels Bohr won the Nobel prize for this discovery, it wasn't too long thereafter that a more complicated picture of the atom emerged as physicists embraced the idea that small particles such as electrons could be treated as if they were electromagnetic waves. In 1925 Erwin Schrödinger (1887–1961) proposed his wave equation, a mathematical expression that causes most first-year chemistry students to glaze over:

$$-\frac{\hbar^2}{2m}\frac{\partial^2 \psi}{\partial x^2} + V(x)\Psi = i\hbar \frac{\partial \psi}{\partial t}$$

Without getting too deep into the weeds, the Schrödinger Equation is a second-order differential equation that describes the total energy of a system as the sum of its kinetic and potential energies. Solutions to this equation for the one-electron atom are many and no one quite knows what to make of the resulting wave functions, especially since they contain the imaginary number i. They must be further manipulated mathematically and graphed in three dimensions to reveal the shapes of the orbitals around the atom where there is a probability of finding an electron.

In my laboratory I illustrate the Bohr model of hydrogen by swinging a tennis ball on a string around my head. The string serves as the coulombic force of attraction that keeps the ball from flying off into space. The constant flick of my wrist supplies the energy for the centripetal force that maintains the ball's acceleration. The solutions to the Schrödinger Equation are best demonstrated with pictures, a 3-D computer simulation, or balloons fashioned into the shapes of the various atomic orbitals.

C. S. Lewis lived during this exciting era of scientific advances in atomic theory. He compared the inadequacy of pictures to explain the complex mathematical expressions governing atomic theory to Christ's death on the cross for the atonement of sin, arguing that a man's inability to fathom completely the doctrine of salvation by faith could not be a valid argument for rejecting the gospel. This all makes for a beautiful faith integration. Writing in *Mere Christianity* Lewis says,

> What [scientists] do when they want to explain the atom or something of that sort is to give you a description out of which you can make a mental picture. But then they warn you that this picture is not what the scientists actually believe. The pictures are there only to help you understand the formula. . . . The thing itself cannot be pictured; it can only be expressed mathematically. We are in the same boat here. We believe that the death of Christ is just that point in history at which something absolutely unimaginable from outside shows through into our own world. And if we cannot picture even the

atoms of which our own world is built, of course we are not going to be able to picture this.[9]

We accept many things without fully understanding the *why* or the *how*. Lewis offers the example of enjoying a meal without fully understanding how that food nourishes us and adds, "A man can accept what Christ has done without knowing how it works."[10] Why is it that the literal blood of Jesus Christ had to be shed to forgive sin? Lewis says on its face it is a "very silly theory" and "if God was prepared to let us off, why on earth did He not do so?"[11]

In *Christ-Centered Preaching*, Bryan Chapell draws a similar analogy: "In some ways, the whole process [of preaching] seems ridiculous. To think that eternal destinies will change simply because we voice thoughts from an ancient text more than challenges common sense."[12] Are these not echoes of Paul's characterization of the preaching of the cross as "foolishness" (1 Cor 1:21)? Taken in their proper context, Lewis, Chapell, and the apostle Paul are all arguing that the power of God's word, based on Christ's atonement, is effectual for the salvation of man apart from our understanding of its inner workings.

Lewis concludes, "That is Christianity. That is what has to be believed. Any theories we build up as to how Christ's death did all of this are, in my view, quite secondary: mere plans or diagrams to be left alone if they do not help us, and, even if they do help us, not to be confused with the thing itself."[13] We may not fully comprehend why an innocent man—the Son of God—had to come to earth, live a sinless life, and be put to death on a Roman cross so that we, by a simple act of faith, can be born again, saved from our sins and from eternal damnation.

That I can tease out the gospel from observing a glowing sample of hydrogen gas in an enclosed glass tube to which has

---

9. Lewis, *Mere Christianity*, 55.
10. Lewis, *Mere Christianity*, 55.
11. Lewis, *Mere Christianity*, 56.
12. Chapell, *Christ-Centered Preaching*, 20.
13. Lewis, *Mere Christianity*, 55–56.

been applied an electric field makes for an unforgettable faith integration for my students.[14]

HEAT LOST = HEAT GAINED

The joule is a measure of heat about one-fourth as large as a calorie. It is named after James Joule, whose quotation appears as the epigram to this chapter. In a procedure where we measure a property of metals called the "specific heat," students are taught to remember "heat lost equals heat gained." The specific heat of a substance is like a fingerprint, especially for metals. If one knows the specific heat of an unknown metal, its identity can be narrowed down substantially. We measure the specific heat of different metal samples indirectly by measuring the increase in heat of a known quantity of room temperature water into which a known mass of metal at 100°C is dropped. The amount of heat the metal loses is equal to the amount of heat the water gains. When the system finally achieves equilibrium, it's a simple calculation to find the specific heat of the metal.

This lab makes for a perfect faith integration with Phil 3:7, "But whatever gain I had, I counted as loss for the sake of Christ."

SPEAK UP FOR THOSE WHO HAVE NO VOICE

Sometimes faith integration takes students down the path of social responsibility. The following example shows one way this happens. In one of the laboratory classes I teach, students learn techniques to separate heterogenous mixtures of solids. One procedure involves the separation of sodium chloride from beach sand by mixing the solid mixture in water, filtering the resulting slurry to remove the sand and evaporating the water to recover the sodium chloride. Laboratory scale separation techniques remind me of my first job after graduate school. I held a position as an environmental

---

14. For another example of a faith integration that borders on the *Twilight Zone* or the *Matrix*, see Rummo, "Are We Living?"

chemist at a chemical manufacturing plant in upstate New York. We used similar techniques in the plant but on a much larger scale. I learned many things at that first job; among them, I learned that, despite a tome of federal, state, and local regulations, a chemical manufacturing plant is not one of the most pleasant places in the world to work. And this is in America.

Near the end of this laboratory class, I ask my students to hold up their cellphones. Not surprisingly, every student has one. I ask them if they know anything about the batteries that power them and, more pointedly, if they know where the raw materials come from.

They are shocked when I pull back the curtain, so to speak, to reveal to them that, in addition to the lithium, the batteries also contain the metal cobalt. Sixty percent of the world's supply of cobalt is mined in the Congo, dug out of the ground by hand, most often by children who are forced into open-pit mines, sometimes at gunpoint. An article in the *Washington Post* in 2016 titled "The Cobalt Pipeline"[15] detailed the terrible plight of the young "creuseurs," or diggers, as they risk their lives so the rest of the world can benefit from the latest technology offered by electric vehicles and cellphone manufacturers using the lithium-cobalt batteries in their products.

I had created a discussion-group post for this lab that included a link to the *Washington Post* article as well as three other articles that explained the technology behind the production of lithium-cobalt batteries and the amount of extra energy expended in their manufacture. Three students weighed in with their comments. One wrote,

> I think we often, myself included, reap the benefits of the materials and ingredients we come in possession of without considering at all where it came from, or what we are endorsing by purchasing these items. It is not a common thought of mine to wonder if a child labored for hours on end, unpaid and treated unfairly, to bring me a new cell phone that I definitely don't need. It is the duty of a Christian chemist to work to help those who need it, which in the lab may look like developing new ways for

---

15. Frankel, "Cobalt Pipeline."

our phone to be small and still powerful. We cannot in good conscience use our gifts and the skills we learn for selfish or superfluous ends knowing the call we have as Christians to help the less fortunate and to use our gifts for the glory of God.[16]

In *Desiring the Kingdom*, James K. A. Smith explains that consumerism necessitates this type of invisibility. He calls it "a learned ignorance." Using the example of a clothing store in a mall he writes,

> They don't want us to ask, "Where does all this stuff come from?" Instead, they encourage us to accept a certain magic, the myth that the garments and equipment that circulate from the mall into our homes and into the landfill simply emerged in shops as if dropped by aliens. The process of production and transport remain hidden and invisible. This invisibility is not accidental; it is necessary in order not to see that this way of life is unsustainable and selfishly lives off of the backs of the majority of the world.[17]

Scripture commands us not only to speak up for those who have no voice but to judge righteously, and to defend the rights of the poor and needy (Prov 31:9 NIV). Jesus said, "Everyone to whom much was given, of him much will be required" (Luke 12:48). Those of us who have been blessed with an abundance—certainly living in America almost guarantees that when compared to the rest of the world—have an obligation to first make ourselves aware of the plight of the less fortunate; but it doesn't stop with awareness. It then becomes our responsibility to act. We should seek ways to be lavishly generous with our own resources and to "do justice and to love kindness" as we walk humbly with our God (Mic 6:8). As scientists, we have a cultural mandate to be responsible for earth and its people. John Frame writes, "Man is to use the resources of the world but is not to exploit or deplete them."[18] Where reasonable, Christians should support environmental

---

16. Rummo, "Teaching Science Students," para. 18. Other students' posts are included in this essay.

17. Smith, *Desiring the Kingdom*, 101.

18. Frame, *Doctrine of the Christian Life*, 744.

policies that intelligently manage the earth's natural resources without causing economic harm to people.

SUMMARY

In this chapter I shared several detailed examples of laboratory procedures I teach to both cohorts of chemistry students that allow for imaginative faith integrations. Hands-on experiments add another dimension to the learning experience and provide a rich trove of material for memorable faith integrations, provided the instructor is creative and sufficiently versed in Scripture to make a meaningful connection between science and theology. The collaborative and interactionist view of natural science and biblical faith states that "both the natural sciences and theology have something to say about the universe. There is no intrinsic contradiction between them insomuch as they are properly articulated."[19] As leaders in Christian institutions of higher education, it is our God-given responsibility to affirm this harmonious view of the marriage between natural science and our faith. For those within the pure sciences, this may mean entertaining the types of questions and discussions raised herein, but the bigger lesson is for all educators in all disciplines. Not every professor of higher education has the option of a laboratory component in a course. That means he or she must find creative alternatives such as videos, models, or course-specific workshops outside of the regular lecture. As we look for opportunities to integrate faith into the courses we teach, it is important that we articulate them properly, using excellent visuals that will leave lasting gospel impressions on the minds of our students.

The teaching of Scripture apart from science is also one of my joys at PBA. In the next chapter, I will share my experiences leading "Keller's Kids," a Chapel Life Group for students that I have been leading for the past two semesters.

---

19. Haines, "Does Science Conflict?," 68.

CHAPTER SIX

"Keller's Kids"

If you have Bible-believing young people in your church [or small group], you may have the best generation of evangelists in a culture that is going the other way. It is remarkable what young people, committed to Christ, are willing to say or do.

—BRYAN CHAPELL[1]

INTRODUCTION

PALM BEACH ATLANTIC UNIVERSITY was blessed with a record enrollment for the fall 2022 semester. The sheer number of incoming freshmen overwhelmed parking, residence halls, internet bandwidth, the dining hall, and regular chapel services. The School of Ministry responded to the need for more chapel opportunities by creating Chapel Life Groups (CLG). These were small, faculty-led Bible studies for the students. The idea was to provide additional opportunities outside of the regular, larger chapel gatherings,

---

1. Chapell, "Evangelistic Preaching."

while still allowing students to receive chapel credit. I was among the dozen or so faculty members who were asked to lead a group. In this chapter I will share my experiences leading a weekly CLG as a model for other professors teaching at Christian institutions of higher education. Hopefully what I share here will be helpful to them to model a small group Bible study on their campus. To that end, I include our School of Ministry's guidelines, a short history of small group Bible studies and their effectiveness, the material I ultimately decided to use for my group, and how I arrived at the name, "Keller's Kids."

WHENCE CAME "SMALL GROUPS"?

When I first became a born-again Christian, I joined an independent Baptist church where I learned about several additional types of weekly meetings that were common in evangelical churches during the twentieth century. One of them was Sunday school. The tradition persists to this day, but in some churches the name has been dropped in favor of "small groups." Small groups are similar to Sunday school in that they are created to reach a specific age group or life stage. In most evangelical churches there are groups for married couples, singles, college-age students, middle and high schoolers, and younger children. Sunday school and small groups differ in that the latter are less formal and not limited to meeting on Sundays or in the church building, but often are hosted in people's homes where the atmosphere is more relaxed.

We were way ahead of the times at that small, independent Baptist church where I went as a new believer. One of the deacons had started a small group he named "the adult fellowship." It met weekly on Mondays at different homes in the community. It wasn't just a Bible study—there was a time of prayer, questions and answers, and fellowship. There was also food, lots of food. The impression those wonderful Christians made on me remains some forty-five years later. It was the most effective method for teaching the Bible that I have experienced in a church to date.

Therefore, I shouldn't be surprised at the effectiveness of studying Scripture in a small group setting. The church of the first century was essentially a small group. Paul used the Greek word *ekklesia*, which, prior to the birth of Christianity, meant "any gathering of a group of people."[2] In the early days of the church, meetings were small, around thirty people. Some sources contend that it wasn't until the third century when actual church buildings began to be built.[3]

On Christian college campuses, the small group phenomenon is nothing new. Organizations such as InterVarsity, The Navigators, and Cru (formerly Campus Crusade for Christ) have been offering leadership training to faculty and students on college campuses for decades to help them start ministries to reach students with the gospel.[4] Students themselves have also been known to start small worship groups spontaneously, a phenomenon I have observed on our campus.

FIRST EXPERIENCES LEADING A CHAPEL LIFE GROUP (CLG)

When I was asked to lead a Chapel Life Group, I jumped at the opportunity. I had led a small group Bible study for young married couples on Sundays and Wednesdays at my former church in New Jersey, and remembered the impact that it had in the lives of the couples who attended.

---

2. Coffman, "Where Did Small Groups Start?"
3. Coffman, "Where Did Small Groups Start?"
4 These three para-church organizations offer a wealth of resources for starting a small group Bible study to both students and faculty: "InterVarsity is a vibrant campus ministry that establishes and advances witnessing communities of students and faculty"(Intervarsity.org). "Since 1933, the Navigators have helped people in over 100 countries bring hope and purpose to others through something we call Life-to-Life discipleship. It's not a program or curriculum, it's more of a commitment to help our friends know Jesus, starting from wherever they are in life" (Navigators.org). Cru offers leadership and discipleship training, mission trips, careers, and one-year full-time internships (Cru.org).

I had already been handing out *Beginning a Praying Life*,[5] by Paul Miller, to students who came by my office. As previously mentioned in chapter 3, making Christian books available to students is one of the ways I reach out to them with the gospel through hospitality. Despite teaching at a Christian university, I wasn't sure where students were with their prayer lives. Whenever I had students come by my office for help with their chemistry homework, especially those who were struggling with the material, and I asked them if they were praying *and* studying, they often looked at me as if I had two heads.

PBA's School of Ministry provided faculty with a one-page set of guidelines explaining how they wanted us to conduct the CLG meetings.[6] We all met together for a one-hour informational meeting in the lounge area of the School of Ministry—including members of the faculty who were chosen, the chapel director, CM Global's director Mark Kaprive, and his staff. The ensuing discussion dealt with the details of how they wanted us to conduct our CLGs. We were told to try and limit our talking to 30 percent of the time and allow the students 70 percent. It was clear that this was to be more of a discussion and less of a lecture. Topics for the groups were suggested. Some faculty had already decided on the material they would use. My selection of Miller's book was approved, and Chapel Life Groups began as an experiment in the spring 2023 semester.

I knew getting started was going to be slow. I am a chemistry professor, and the group announcement listing the subject

---

5. This title is available as both a short, fifty-seven-page booklet titled *Beginning a Praying Life* and the longer, 304-page version, *A Praying Life*.

6. The guidelines were very precise: I. Welcome, introduction and opening prayer (3–5 minutes) II. Announcements and highlights (2–4 min.) III. Debrief of previous study and forecast of future study (5 min.) IV. Share any "God stories" (2–4 min.) V. Reading of Scripture related to message or book study (2–4 min.) VI. Discovery questions and discussion based on the passage (25 min.) VII. Prayer requests (2–4 min.) VIII. Closing prayer (5 min.) IX. *Attended* scans (5 min.) X. Any feedback from the CLG leader was to be sent to the office of Chapel Ministries.

"Beginning a Praying Life" must have been cause for some head scratching among students that had no idea who I was.

Seven students attended the first meeting. Since we had nothing to talk about from the previous week, it was an awkward start. Fortunately, there were a few students that were currently in one of my classes and they sparked some lively conversation near the end of the hour. I asked them to read the booklet I had handed out. We prayed, and I encouraged them to come back the following week. Rather than meet in a classroom, I changed the venue to the area outside my office where there was more comfortable seating and a nice assortment of free snacks close at hand. More students began showing up. We finished Miller's booklet by the fourth week and I handed out used copies of the longer paperback I had purchased from online sellers of used books.[7] The numbers slowly increased into the teens and we outgrew the area outside my office, forcing us to move back into a classroom. New students began to show up, and others didn't return or didn't attend every week, making it difficult to maintain a discussion with any semblance of continuity. We ended the semester with close to thirty students.

In addition to having given out Miller's booklet to every student that attended—and over twenty copies of the longer, 304-page paperback—I had also offered small, blank notebooks to students who promised they would begin to write down specific requests, date them, and then pray daily, watching to see God's hand in answer to their prayers. It was during finals week when one of the students approached me in the dining hall. He shared with me that he had started writing down specific requests with dates and already had seen God's answer to some of them. "This is unbelievable!" he said. "If I knew this was going to happen, I would have started doing this a lot sooner!"

"The important thing is you're doing it now," I said. "Keep it up!" This casual encounter and others like it are important to me,

---

7. Online sellers of discounted and used Christian books that I have purchased from include: Thriftbooks, Christian Books Discount, ABE Books, The Gospel Coalition Bookstore, and Christian Used Books. Amazon has also been helpful.

as I have no quantitative metric to judge success other than my attendance records. What is helpful are those students who attend faithfully, week after week, and are engaged in the readings and discussions, not just showing up to earn chapel credit.

Despite their encouragement and appreciation, I still felt I hadn't really connected with their deep-seated spiritual needs. Prayer is certainly an important aspect of the Christian life. But not every student at a Christian university is a Christian, and among those that are, some struggle with their identity and the broad concept of the gospel as a way of life, not just as a one-time decision, the result of having prayed the sinner's prayer in Sunday school at their home church when they were children.

GEN Z'S CRISIS OF IDENTITY

Identity is one of the biggest struggles that Gen Z is facing today. But this crisis is a symptom of a deeper crisis. It is a failure to recognize the *imago Dei*. The *imago Dei* is the ultimate definer of our identity. "When we think of identity in this way, it becomes clear that in order to understand who we are, we need to look to the One whose image we bear."[8] But this doesn't happen until first, a person knows God personally, and that begins and continues with the gospel. Sara Barratt Starkey, editor-in-chief of theRebelution.com and the author of *Stand Up, Stand Strong: A Call to Bold Faith in a Confused Culture*, writes:

> Gen Z is a generation of people desperate to know and express themselves. Gen Z is also the most accepting of all "identities" and the most fluid with the concept of identity. We can be whoever we want, regardless of gender, and we are whomever and whatever we feel, regardless of reality. You would assume in this environment of acceptance and encouragement of all identities, that identity crises would be nonexistent. Finally, everyone can be exactly who and what they want to be. But in truth, instead of the most secure and confident generation, much of

8. Starkey, "Gen Z's Identity Crisis," para. 10.

Gen Z is often rootless, aimless, insecure, and desperate to discover who they really are.[9]

If Gen Z is to resolve its identity crisis, it must be confronted with the gospel. They must learn through explicit teaching from the Bible that the gospel is the only means to recognize their identity is in Christ, through a personal relationship with him. I wanted to address this directly through the study of the Scriptures, in addition to what I was doing in my chemistry classes indirectly through faith integration assignments. Leading a CLG would provide the perfect opportunity for me to accomplish this goal.

THE FREEDOM OF SELF-FORGETFULNESS

I recently read *The Freedom of Self-Forgetfulness* by Timothy Keller. I was familiar with his ministry through his podcast, *Gospel in Life*, and as a supporter I received a different book authored by Dr. Keller each month. I had received two copies of this book, one to read, one to give away, and was so impressed by its simple yet profound message for young people I ordered fifty copies in bulk from Christian Book Distributors. This was one of the books I mentioned in chapter 3 that I had been giving away to students that dropped by my office.

This topic was too important to be left to just handing out booklets from my office, and I decided *The Freedom of Self-Forgetfulness* would be the book we would study and discuss over the first five weeks of the fall 2023 semester. It is a short read: three chapters, forty-six pages, including a page with thoughts and questions for reflections. It is a Bible study on the topic of self-esteem from 1 Cor 3:21–4:7. Keller writes that 1 Corinthians "gives us an approach to self-regard, to the self and of seeing ourselves in a way absolutely different from both traditional and modern/postmodern contemporary cultures."[10] Keller explains that the human ego

---

9. Starkey, "Gen Z's Identity Crisis," para. 2.
10. Keller, *Freedom of Self-Forgetfulness*, 12.

is empty, painful, busy, and fragile.[11] He quotes Søren Kierkegaard (1813–1855) who said, "The normal state of the human heart is to try and build its identity around something besides God."[12] This is the sin of the first Adam, rejecting the all-sufficiency of God and instead choosing to run his own life. It is also the sin of every one of us. It is pride, it is *incurvatus in se*, a Latin phrase for living inward for oneself instead of outwardly towards others.

During the five weeks we studied this book, we contrasted the idolatry of self with the image of God from such verses as Eph 2:10, which says that God has made us "masterpieces" created for good works, and Ps 139:14–16 where the psalmist wrote we are "fearfully and wonderfully made" and that God has a plan for our lives, all our days having been written in a book. The students appreciated this study, and some of their comments appear at the end of this chapter.

Word was slowly getting out as evidenced by the slow increase in the number of attendees and, more importantly, those who returned each week. Now that I had addressed Gen Z's identity crisis head-on with five weeks of Bible study aimed directly at this issue, I decided the next book we would read and discuss together would be Keller's *Prodigal God*.

Prodigal God presents an explicit portrayal of God's love, mercy, and grace through the compassion of a father towards both of his wayward sons. In Keller's non-traditional approach to one of the best-known parables in the New Testament, he illustrates the gospel vividly by contrasting the two brothers—the younger, an obvious rebel, with the older—which serves as a metaphor for the self-righteous Pharisees of Jesus' day who were trusting in legalism to save them. Keller says both were wrong, and offers a third way, the gospel, as the only means for knowing our identity and establishing a true relationship with God, our father.

---

11. Keller, *Freedom of Self-Forgetfulness*.
12. Quoted in Keller, *Freedom of Self-Forgetfulness*, 15.

PRODIGAL GOD AS A MEANS TO UNDERSTANDING THE GOSPEL

We began each week in the study of *Prodigal God* by reading Luke 15 in its entirety from a different version of the Bible. Especially memorable was this chapter from *The Message* where it describes the father's feast as "barbecued beef" (Luke 15:27). By studying this book together, it allowed me to share Scriptures with my students that I had learned from Knox Theological Seminary's doctoral class on Paul's Epistle to the Romans. We discussed the doctrines of justification and sanctification, and the importance of good works *after* salvation, not as a means *to* salvation. In this regard, we read and discussed Rom 4:3 and compared it to Jas 2:24. When students asked if a Christian can still sin, we discussed Luther's statement *simul justus et peccator*.[13]

The discussions were spirited. One student asked me what the difference was between a Christian and a Roman Catholic (I tried to answer as diplomatically as I could). Another wanted to know what constituted good works, which led to a discussion of Rom 14:23 ("Whatever does not come from faith is sin") and some chalk work on the blackboard that showed God's love descending from heaven to save us and that love continuing to empower our faith to do good works.

Attendance continued to increase, dropped off during midterm week, and then resumed its growth. We were running out of space in the conference room where we were meeting. Students were sitting on the floor and standing in the back row.

The penultimate week of classes, thirty students showed up. It was the meeting before the Thanksgiving break, and I decided to play the song "Home" by Daughtry as a poignant reminder of where most of us were headed. But the lyrics of the song also paint a picture of the musings of the prodigal son, regretting his decision to leave home, until ultimately repenting and realizing the father's advice that he should have been careful what he had wished for. Before playing it, I asked how many had heard the song before.

---

13. Sproul, "Simul Justus et Peccator."

"KELLER'S KIDS"

Almost no one had. As the song began, I watched the expressions on their faces. They listened reverently. It was an emotional experience, and a fitting way to bring to a conclusion our reading and discussion of *Prodigal God*.

We all long for home. It is one facet of the *imago Dei*. Despite the younger brother's rebellious lifestyle, ultimately he could not continue running from his father's love, nor shake the desire to return home.

Writing on this deep-seated desire that God placed in all humanity, the C. S. Lewis Institute published an essay in January 2010 titled "Reflections: Longing for Home." The writers stated,

> Somewhere deep within each of us is a desire, a longing for a world very different from our own. It is there first of all because we have been created in the image of God and were intended to live with him in a world of love. Though his image has been defaced by the fall, there are still remnants of it within us. The stunning beauty of a sunset, the awe of starry heavens, a deeply moving story or poem, can arouse within us for a brief moment an awareness and desire for our true home.[14]

For the Christian, the desire for home is even stronger. God has placed eternity into the hearts of those who have made Jesus their savior.[15] C. S. Lewis himself echoed these thoughts in his essay "The Weight of Glory":

> In speaking of this desire for our own far-off country, which we find in ourselves even now, I feel a certain shyness. I am almost committing an indecency. I am trying to rip open the inconsolable secret in each one of you—the secret which hurts so much that you take your revenge on it by calling it names like Nostalgia and Romanticism and Adolescence; the secret also which pierces with such sweetness that when, in very intimate conversation, the mention of it becomes imminent, we grow awkward and

---

14. C. S. Lewis Institute, "Reflections: Longing for Home," para. 1.
15. C. S. Lewis Institute, "Reflections: Longing for Home."

affect to laugh at ourselves; the secret we cannot hide and cannot tell, though we desire to do both.[16]

The final week of classes (and the last chance to get chapel credit) forced us into a nearby lecture hall that seats seventy-eight. Close to one hundred students showed up. This was an extraordinary event, and I used the hour not only to review and wrap up our discussion of *Prodigal God*, but to present the plan of salvation using a well-known gospel tool called "3 Circles."[17] After the class was over and most of the students had left, several lingered and asked questions about the Bible. I left with a deeper appreciation of the hunger of these students for answers, which they can find only in the gospel. Am I willing to provide these answers to them? The Lord whispered, "Whom shall I send?" My answer is "Here am I, send me!" (Isa 6:8).

SUMMARY WITH STUDENT REFLECTIONS

In this chapter I shared my experiences leading a Chapel Life Group as an alternate experience to the regular chapel the university offers. Through a combination of patience, prayer, and encouragement from a handful of my students, and a selection of relevant material aimed at the challenges Gen Z faces, the group bonded. Below in table 7 is a summary list of the material I used over the course of two semesters in my CLG and a brief description of each.

---

16. Lewis, *Weight of Glory*, 4–5.
17. Scroggins, "3 Circles."

"KELLER'S KIDS"

Table 7 List of Materials Used in "Keller's Kids"

Beginning a Praying Life, Paul Miller	A short devotional booklet on cultivating prayer as a daily, intentional discipline of the Christian life
A Praying Life, Paul Miller	A longer book by the same author offering a more detailed description of what a praying life looks like
The Freedom of Self-Forgetfulness, Timothy Keller	A short, three-chapter booklet that offers a path to true Christian joy through exploring a Christian's true identity in Christ
Prodigal God, Timothy Keller	A different take on the parable of the prodigal son examines the legalism of the elder brother, the bohemian lifestyle of his younger brother, why both were wrong, and the gracious father who loved them both
Beyond Boundaries, Timothy Keller	The inclusivity and exclusivity of the gospel

Measuring outcomes is not necessarily a function of numbers. Chapel at PBA is treated like a class, and students are required to attend twenty-four chapels per year. Many students wait until the end of the semester to satisfy this requirement and as a result, the huge jump in attendance during the last week of classes is almost certainly due in part to this phenomenon. Nonetheless, what follows is a graph (graph 1) of attendance to my CLG, beginning in February, during the early stages of the spring 2023 through the end of the fall 2023 semester.[18] We began reading and discussing *The Freedom of Self-Forgetfulness* on August 31.

While numbers of attendees may tell us something, student comments, although qualitative, are a better assessment of outcomes. I had several casual conversations with students from my CLG in the dining hall. Some of these conversations were simply expressions of gratitude, enquiries if I would be teaching an actual

---

18. This graph is a reconstruction of e-mails, photos of the groups I took, and Facebook posts. The long, flat plateau between April and August is the summer break when we didn't meet.

Bible class at some future point, or questions about the material we had discussed.

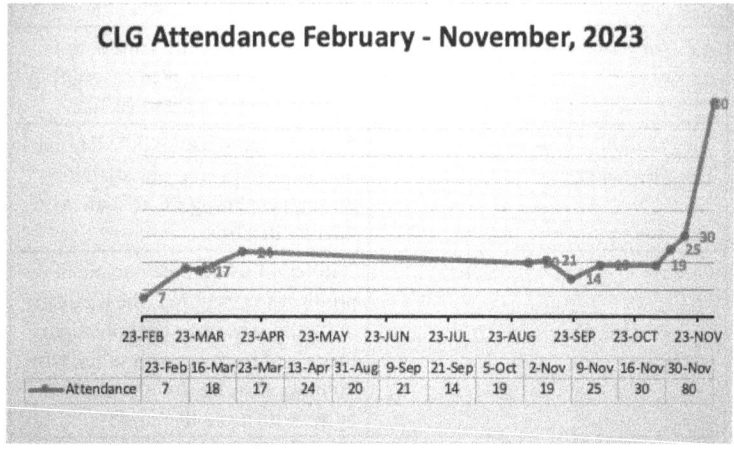

Graph 1: CLG Attendance, February–November 2023

I sent an email to a list of students who had attended faithfully during the semester, asking them for their impressions of the group. Two replied in lengthy emails, excerpts of which I am sharing below with their permission.

> The introduction of the chapel life group was both a unique and a transformative experience. One thing I have thoroughly enjoyed about being in "Keller's Kids" is how, as a small, intimate group, we have been able to dive deeply into the material as we study the Keller books and dissect a Bible story in detail. As we expand on a concept over the course of several weeks, I have been able to sit on and "marinate" in the message . . . and more readily make applications of what we are studying to my daily college life. I have found that I have not only drawn closer to the friends I have invited to attend, I have also made new friendships that have been both spiritually enriching and have provided me with much needed support through the challenging college experience. In addition, I have noticed in both myself and in others, that

we are able to openly discuss even difficult subjects and ask difficult questions because of the trust and support we have established with each other. I found that it truly became something I was looking forward to every week in the midst of the chaos and stress of the semester.

The other student sent a bullet-point list which I am including below. This student "prophesied" that we were going to need a bigger room. She was right. This is how she was impacted:

- Building connections with other students desiring to grow deeper with the Lord.

- Receiving encouragement at times when I need it. Sharing encouragement to others to be light/salt of the earth.

- Being led by a leader who knows me and is willing to fight alongside me in faith. I'm not exactly sure how to explain this further, but it's the most important reason for me. I'm in no way speaking against the larger chapel services, however many times I feel unseen and only fulfilling an obligation I must keep. The structure and material we discuss in Keller's kids allows me to ask questions, share testimonies, exercise my faith, and genuinely grow spiritually at PBA. Not only is the atmosphere important for a growth in faith, but also the people who walk alongside you (which is why many times I prefer a small group setting as opposed to a large chapel service on campus).

- Discussions relevant to Gen Z that make us think outside of the box. *The Freedom of Self-Forgetfulness* was a very interesting way to start within the group, but it was necessary. Many of us students needed to hit that reset button when it comes to our pursuit of faith. Walking humbly and genuinely in our identity in Christ are things not often confronted in Gen Z (many times the gospel that is preached to us does not require a transformation of the "self").

- Last but not least is the prayer requests. I wholeheartedly believe that prayer changes everything. At Keller's Kids I not only took part in it, but also shared in the joy of testimonies that resulted from our requests to the Lord.

Both of these students' comments were insightful. They support the findings not only of my own research, but also the preliminary results from a survey being conducted at Baylor University on the effectiveness of CLGs in comparison to the larger chapel experience.[19]

Moving forward, during the spring 2024 semester I am planning to continue focusing on the gospel in its broad understanding by beginning with a new Keller book *Beyond Boundaries*. This short read is a three-point sermon on Philip's encounter with the Ethiopian eunuch recorded in Acts 8:26–40. Its message highlights both the inclusivity and exclusivity of the gospel. After this, my plan is to read and discuss the lengthier Keller book *Encounters with Jesus*. In the next chapter, I will explain how I help fulfill the third part of PBA's motto, "extending hands," through an exciting opportunity for students to distribute Bibles in Peru to the indigenous Quechua living in the high-altitude valleys of the Andes Mountains.

---

19. I discuss some of these preliminary findings in the final chapter of this project.

CHAPTER SEVEN

Modeling Evangelism for Gen Z through Missions

Jesus Christ the Son of God [is] the final and decisive Word of God to men; that in Him alone is the certainty of salvation given to men; that this Gospel must be preached to every living human soul.

—STEPHEN NEILL (1900–1984)[1]

Christianity and missions. The two are inseparably linked. . . . The command to go forth with the good news [is] the very heart of the faith.

—RUTH A. TUCKER[2]

---

1. Neill, *History of Christian Missions*, 417. The author is writing about the theological unanimity among participants at the Edinburgh Conference of 1910.

2. Tucker, *From Jerusalem to Irian Jaya*, 25.

INTRODUCTION

IN THIS CHAPTER I will explain how I fulfill, in part, the third part of PBA's motto, "extending hands," by offering a unique opportunity to my students to promote Scripture in the Peruvian Andes. This short-term mission trip fulfills their workshop requirement for the entire academic year, as well as giving them the opportunity for a "hands-on, active approach to learning" about missions by actively practicing evangelism.[3] It also allows me to model how to share their faith, "something that is not being modeled for Gen Z."[4] For the last three years, a group of students has accompanied me on a ten-day trek through the Peruvian Andes where we promote Scripture distribution among the indigenous Quechua. It is an adventuresome trek, featuring long walks during the day and freezing cold nights camped in tents. We accompany our host family, the Yanacs,[5] whom I have known for almost twenty-five years. They are full-time missionaries with Wycliffe Bible Translators. Together, with members of Asociación Alli Willaqui (AWI)[6]—a local, Quechua, evangelistic organization—we visit a half dozen villages along a unique trekking circuit every year, distributing Bibles and Bible story books translated into the Quechuas' heart language. In what follows, I will explain the tedious process of how the Huaylas Quechua translation came to be, how I became involved in Scripture promotion, the necessity for foreign missions, the effectiveness of short-term mission trips, and why such trips should be a part of any leader's ministry at a Christian University for the sake of their Gen Z students.

---

3. "The majority of Gen Z teens prefer a hands-on, active approach to learning." Feed, "What We Know About Gen Z."

4. "Fewer than 1 in 5 Christian parents in the US believe the youth group their teen is attending is equipping them to talk about their faith with others." Barna and Impact 360, *Gen Z*, 26.

5. Ade and Rachel Yanac, serving with Wycliffe Bible Translators. https://www.wycliffe.org/partner/Yanac.

6. awiperu.com/es.

HOW IT ALL STARTED IN ANCASH, PERU: *TRABAJO EN EQUIPO*[7]

In 1964, Wycliffe Bible Translators began a program to translate the Bible into the Huaylas dialect of Quechua, the language spoken in Peru's Callejón de Huaylas, the huge valley that splits the Andes into two separate ranges, the Cordillera Blanca and the Cordillera Negra. Two women, Helen Larsen and Margie Levengood, began the tedious work of translation. In 1970, just six years after the work had begun, a devastating earthquake occurred off the coast of Peru. In what has been called the worst natural disaster in the Western Hemisphere during the twentieth century, the earthquake unleashed an enormous landslide. The rocks and ice which slid off Nevado Huascarán, Peru's highest mountain, swept through the village of Yungay, killing seventy thousand people.[8] The two translators were accused of being witches and blamed "for having brought a new religion to the valley."[9] They continued to work for several more years until both left Peru. In the years which followed, new people joined the team including linguists, literacy specialists, and others who worked in support of the translators. Three Quechua-speaking Peruvian nationals—Timoteo Trejo, Prospero Colonia, and Leopoldo Rodriguez—also joined the team and assisted the translators with the readability of the translation.

The Huaylas version of the New Testament was finally dedicated in 2007, some forty-three years after the work had begun. Several years later, the Old Testament translation was completed along with translations of the entire Bible in two other Quechua dialects spoken in the region. We now have translations of the entire Bible in the three dialects of Quechua spoken in the Ancash region of Peru.

---

7. *Trabajo en Equipo* is Spanish for "teamwork."
8. Britannica, "Ancash Earthquake of 1970."
9. Delaware Bible Church, "History of the Quechua Bible Translation." Rachel Yanac provided the narration; I appear in this video around the 7:45–7:50 mark.

HOW I BECAME INVOLVED IN SCRIPTURE PROMOTION IN THE PERUVIAN ANDES

In 1997, Roy Seals, an independent Baptist missionary and lifelong friend, asked me if I would pray about accompanying him on a two-week mission trip to Venezuela.[10] There were four missionary families he wanted to visit located in four different cities: Barquisimeto, Valencia, Nirgua, and Chajuraña. This last "city" was not a city by western standards, but an Indian village located deep in the Amazon rainforest. It was there that the Vernoy family—Clint, Rita, and their four children—lived among and ministered to a tribe of Yekwana Indians. To get there, we flew from Caracas to Puerto Ayacucho, on the Colombia-Venezuela border. We then boarded a six-seat, single-engine Cessna 206, operated by Mission Aviation Fellowship, for the ninety-minute flight to Chajuraña, landing on a field that the Indians had cleared with machetes from the jungle overgrowth. Every time I have told this story, I conclude it by saying: "When Roy first explained to me what this trip involved, I did what any Bible-believing, KJV-only, red-blooded, flag-waving American male would do. I got down on my knees, and looked up towards heaven . . . into my wife's eyes and I asked her for permission." She said yes, and several months later, in early 1998, I found myself in the jungle with Roy and the Vernoy family. We took part in various activities that included swimming in the Chajura river, accompanying a group of Yekwana in canoes on a hunting trip, a fishing expedition for three-foot long worms in the river bottom, and a village-wide feast to honor us on our last night. That evening, while resting in hammocks in the Vernoy's hut, Roy said, "If you think this has been a great trip, next year we are planning on hiking through the Andes mountains in Peru to take portions of Scripture to unreached Quechua." A year later we were hiking on the Santa Cruz

---

10. Rummo, "God Forsaken—Not!" In *View from the Grass Roots*, 250. The story of this first mission trip to Venezuela was published along with several others in chapter 11, "Missionaries and Missionary Adventures," of my first book. It is currently out of print, but used copies can be purchased from a variety of online booksellers.

trail with two-dozen other guys from the States on what became my first Andes trek. We walked for six days, camping each evening at a different campsite. Most were at altitudes above thirteen thousand feet. During one day's hike, we crossed the continental divide at Punta Union (15,675 feet). Two dozen burros and their *arrieros* (burro managers) carried all of the heavier gear. Each day, we stopped in a village along the route where we were able to hand out portions of Scripture in both Spanish and Huaylas Quechua. The New Testament translation had not been completed in 1999, the year of this first trek. When it was over, I was physically exhausted. Back home I stepped on the bathroom scale and realized I had lost ten pounds. I promised myself I'd never do this again.

Fortunately, God is patient with our foolishness and has a sense of humor. Two years later I was back in Ancash County, Peru, hiking on a different route with a different group of men and women from the States. On this trip, our hosts were now regularly featuring a nightly showing of the *Jesus Film*[11] in the Huaylas Quechua dialect in every village where we camped. We also had more books of the New Testament translated to distribute, including the Gospel of John.

Over the past twenty-four years I have trekked through the Peruvian Andes on Scripture promotion treks a total of twenty times. I have come to know and love the group of dedicated, full-time missionaries and evangelists who live in Huaraz, making this outreach possible year-round. The ministry has grown from when we had very few portions of Scripture in just one Quechua dialect to now having completed translations of the entire Bible in the three dialects spoken in this region.[12]

The guide who led us on that first trek in 1999, Adelid Yanac, was moved by this "group of twenty-five gringos from the States," as he characterized us. That a bunch of Americans were willing to

11. Krish and Sykes, *Jesus Film*. For more, see Jesus Film Project, A Cru Ministry: "A Christian Media Ministry Bringing Millions Face-to-Face with Jesus In Their Heart Language." www.jesusfilm.org.

12. The three Quechua languages are Huaylas, Northern Conchucos, and Southern Conchucos. They all differ enough to be considered languages, not dialects.

leave their comfort and spend a week in the inhospitable climate of the mountains to reach his people with the gospel was the motivation that led him to walk away from his position as a mountain guide and surrender to full-time missionary work. Adelid has led every Andes trek since.[13]

He married Rachel McDonald, a Wycliffe missionary who had moved from Ohio to Huaraz to teach the missionary kids (MKs) who were there with their parents, assisting in the Bible translations. The Yanacs helped form the local Quechua evangelistic organization, AWI, (*Alli Willaqui*—the "Good News Association"), which has largely taken over the work of Scripture promotion and evangelization throughout the region.

THE EFFECTIVENESS OF SHORT-TERM MISSION TRIPS

Adelid's story—"From Mountain Guide to Evangelist-Trekker"—is not an uncommon after-effect of an Andes trek. I have seen it happen again and again: participants return to the States and, shortly thereafter, surrender to go to Bible college or become involved in some line of ministerial work, including joining a translation project, becoming a pastor, missionary, teacher, evangelist, or join an organization involved in some form of kingdom ministry as a member of the support staff.

God uses many things to call men into full-time ministry, but something special occurs when a person goes on a short-term mission trip and is exposed to a different culture, speaking a different language, in a different part of the world. And if that place is in the developing world, in an "uttermost part" (Acts 1:8) as the King James version of the Bible describes those faraway and often forgotten regions, the impact of the gospel is often more profound. One reason is that the people in these backwaters are usually living

---

13. I find that, often, when we surrender something we love to God's service, he gives it back to us with greater meaning. Adelid is still a mountain guide, but he is guiding trekkers in the ministry of Scripture promotion. He is still fishing; he has just become a "fisher of men" (Matt 4:19).

in poverty and are more receptive to the gospel. In the book of James, the writer explains this phenomenon: "Listen, my beloved brothers, has not God chosen those who are poor in the world to be rich in faith and heirs of the kingdom, which he has promised to those who love him?" (Jas 2:5). We have witnessed this phenomenon in Peru almost every year; the higher the elevation a village is located, the more receptive the people are to the gospel.[14]

I was curious why short-term mission trips are often so "reflective-effective,"[15] and so I asked Roy Seals, who is now the director of Global Faith Mission to help me understand this phenomenon. During an interview, he explained why short-term mission trips can be effective, and why they should be a part of any leader's ministry at a Christian university:

> Fifty years ago, no one went on short terms mission trips. It is a relatively recent phenomenon in missions The first time my dad saw the mission field was when he left to go to the mission field. It is helpful you're not just reading a book, but you can see, touch and taste, impacting all of our senses. It enables us to visualize what a people group is like. It's done a lot for those who are serious about missions to make healthy decisions. It stimulates interest in missions for those who are not called to be career missionaries. It does create promoters of mission work through prayer and giving. For pastors who go, they come back and promote missions like never before. It has also helped the parents of the son or daughter who is going to a mission field. Yes, they can release their son or daughter to a foreign country for mission work. It is also important that students can become lifelong friends and partners in ministry. The negative side of this is that

14. The higher the elevation, the more difficult it is logistically to provide essential municipal services such as electricity, water, safe roads leading to larger towns where people can travel to purchase food and other necessities that they cannot grow on their farms, and adequate health care. At lower elevations, more municipal services have been provided, bringing with them the encroachment of modernity, including cellphones, television, and the internet.

15. "Reflective-effective" is a term I coined to explain the delayed response after returning from one of these trips. It often happens to participants after reflection on the trek days, or weeks after returning to the US.

a short-term trip often doesn't paint an accurate picture of cultural adaptation, living in another place, learning a foreign language fluently. But the positives far outweigh the negative.[16]

It is almost impossible to spend two weeks in a foreign country ministering to a people group and not be impacted deeply. But we must not forget, the people to whom we minister are the priority. It's not about us. The command is to go and teach, baptize, and make disciples (Matt 28:19).

Sowing the seed of the gospel—*Scripture promotion*—is the first step in going and teaching. It is pioneering evangelism. Jesus emphasized the importance of the seed of the gospel and the ground upon which it fell by speaking about it in three of the Gospels: Matt 13, Luke 8, and Mark 4. Paul added his thoughts in 1 Cor 3:6–7: "I planted, Apollos watered, but God gave the growth." We are the sowers. We have a small but important part to play in world evangelism. After a short-term mission trip is over and a group returns, the majority of the work remains to be done. Lest we think too high-mindedly of ourselves, Paul reminds us we are God's servants: "So, neither he who plants, nor he who waters is anything, but only God who gives the growth."

In the letter to the church in Rome, Paul realized that planning a missionary journey to Spain would require prayer and logistical support from his followers. In this next section, I will explain the planning that goes into an Andes trek, including the logistical machine that gets us from south Florida to our first campsite in the mountains, how the students are chosen and raise their support, and finally share a narrative of the 2022 trek.

THE ANATOMY OF AN ANDES TREK

It should be the goal of every professor teaching at a Christian college to model for their students how to share their faith.[17] One

---

16. Roy Seals, FaceTime interview with author, Jan. 3, 2024.
17. "Among American Christian Evangelicals of all ages, opinion is evenly

way to do this is to get involved in the mission program at the university where they teach. Missional involvement could be simply joining students who are already taking part in some missional work, either locally or abroad, and supporting them prayerfully and financially. Whatever the level of involvement, it is important for students to see their professors actively involved in the Great Commission in some form.

When we moved to south Florida in 2017, and I was hired six months later to teach chemistry at Palm Beach Atlantic University, I knew it would not be long before a group of my students and I would be hiking through Peru's Andes Mountains on one of these potentially life-changing trips.

Planning an Andes trek may appear to be a logistical nightmare, and if I were the only person making those plans, it would be. Fortunately, there are many people involved in planning a trip of this magnitude, always months in advance, both here in the States and in Peru.

Participants, in this case interested students, are interviewed by the two student co-leaders for the trip. Once accepted, they then have to raise their own support by writing letters to their home churches, asking mom and dad, working jobs after school, and other creative means. PBA often makes mission scholarships available to students to defray the cost, which is usually around two thousand dollars. Months before departure from the US, the group meets on a regular basis to discuss progress in raising funds, to go over the eight-page guide and checklist I prepared after the first trek in 1999, to make sure everyone's passport is up-to-date, and, most importantly, to pray. Plane tickets have to be purchased for the round-trip flights from south Florida to Lima, Peru's capital city. In-country transportation from Lima to Huaraz and then from Huaraz to wherever we are starting the trek also has to be pre-arranged. Hotel rooms have to be booked. Food for a week

---

divided on the importance of personal evangelism: 53% agree it is very important to personally encourage non-Christians to trust Jesus Christ as their Savior, but 47% disagree. How can young people be expected to share their faith when the adults in their lives may not even see this as important?" Barna and Impact 360, *Gen Z*, 26.

has to be purchased. A cook and an assistant have to be hired to prepare meals during the trek. Our host family takes care of all of the logistics in-country, including mapping the area where we will hike and the villages we will visit. My responsibility is to get our group to the airport in Lima and coordinate some of the details just mentioned. I have done this so many times it now all works like a beautifully choreographed ballet.

In January 2019 I began to plan a trek for later that year which would include several friends from my former church in New Jersey who were experienced, having been on previous Andes treks before. One student from PBA accompanied us along with the CM Global director, Mark Kaprive.[18] Although we had a smaller group that year, it was important to be able to introduce our host missionaries in Peru to the university's missions program director.

The following two years, COVID-19 made international travel impossible. Peru was the hardest hit country with the highest death rate of any other country in the world due to its poor infrastructure, lack of adequate healthcare, and informal economy that forces workers to move from one city to another in search of jobs.[19]

In 2022 we were finally able to plan a trip. In June, I was privileged to introduce a group of nine Palm Beach Atlantic University students to this ministry. We flew from Miami to Lima where our bus was waiting for us in the parking lot at the airport for the eight-hour overnight ride that would take us along the Pan-American Highway at sea level, then climb up the highway that snakes through the Cordillera Negra, topping out at the Conococha Pass at 13,350 feet until beginning its descent to Huaraz where we arrived early the next morning. After taking two days to acclimatize in Huaraz and a third day in Chacas, a village on the other side

---

18. CM Global stands for Campus Ministries Global. "CM Global is aimed at encouraging students to act out of an overflow of God's heart and purposes for peoples of all nations. Our service abroad trips give students the opportunity to share God's love, strengthen their faith, and broaden their perspectives. Previous trips have included: Brazil, Peru, Cambodia, Finland, Greece, South Africa, Haiti, Japan, Thailand, and many more!" Palm Beach, "Campus Ministries and CMGlobal," under CMGlobal.

19. Beaubien, "Peru Has the Highest COVID."

of the Cordillera Blanca, we boarded another bus and set out for Conopa Alta in the northern Conchucos valley where we would spend our first day doing missionary work.

Almost immediately after we arrived, curious locals began to filter into the field at the end of the village outside a school building where our tents had been pitched. A soccer game broke out: It was PBA vs. Peru—at 11,350 feet! (Miraculously, we won!) A group of musicians showed up playing traditional Quechua tunes. We all danced until it was time for dinner, our chef having whipped up an amazing three-course meal in a tent no larger than 150 square feet.

That evening the entire village came out to our campsite to watch the *Jesus Film* in the drafty school building. After the movie one of the AWI evangelists spoke to the crowd. Another played music on a harp and sang a folk tune in the Quechua's native language. Finally, it was our turn. I spoke first in Spanish, explaining who we were and why we had come to Peru. Then, one by one, the rest of the group introduced themselves. Two students spoke Spanish. Adelid translated for the rest into Quechua. Then Conopa Alta's mayor spoke, thanking us for coming, and finally called the names of the adult members from each family who picked their way through the crowd to the front of the room and were presented a Bible by one of the students.

"¡Qué Dios le bendiga!" (May God bless you!) each of us said as we placed a copy of the Bible into each person's hands. "¡Muchas gracias!" was the reply, accompanied by joyful expressions on the faces of all. The meeting ended shortly thereafter. Exhausted, we turned in for the night.

After breakfast the next morning we departed on foot for what was to be a seven-hour hike: first down into the valley below us on a steep, gravel-strewn trail, then up through a mountain pass approaching fourteen thousand feet where we paused some four hours later for lunch and to take in the spectacular view. We continued down the other side to the second village on our circuit, Yegua Corral, where, that evening, we repeated the program. The next day, after another grueling seven-hour walk, we arrived in the village of Carhuacasha where we repeated the program for a third time and subsequently the next evening in the village of Ocshapampa.

We gave out approximately 450 Bibles in those four villages to a people group that God loves as much as he loves you and me. The Quechua in these villages had never seen a copy of the word of God in their own language.

In 2023, another group of nine students and I repeated this performance along a different route in the Huaylas Valley. Similar to the trip a year earlier, we visited five villages. On the way back to Huaraz, our bus stopped a half-dozen times at schools in small villages that dotted the highway. We spoke to the teachers and students and gave them Bibles and Bible story books. On this trip, we were able to distribute almost seven hundred Bibles and one hundred Bible story books.

In 2024, we are planning to return with ten students who have already gone through the interview process and have been accepted by CM Global. Half of them are either in the university's pre-nursing or pre-healthcare track. Because of this, we are planning to add a medical component to the 2024 trek to include distributing reading glasses, vitamins, pain and parasite medication, and conducting vital signs checkups in the villages we will visit. A local registered nurse will accompany us. The emphasis will remain on Scripture promotion, and we will conduct evening showings of the *Jesus Film* in every village as we have always done, followed by a short worship service including music, a gospel message, and an invitation to receive Christ at the close.

Sometimes I wonder how effective placing a Bible into a person's hands can really be. I shouldn't wonder. The Bible says, "The word of God is living and active, sharper than any two-edged sword, piercing to the division of soul and of spirit, of joints and of marrow, and discerning the thoughts and intentions of the heart" (Heb 4:12).

This is God's work, and the members of AWI often return to the villages we visit on our short, ten-day trips. During the rainy season, when they are not hosting Scripture promotion treks, they conduct seminars to train local pastors and conduct meetings in the villages that have churches. And despite follow-up work on their part, along with the small group of evangelical Quechua pastors scattered throughout the region, there remains a dire need for Bible training.

Further complicating the situation is illiteracy. AWI has programs to teach people how to read and write. But owing to the vast distances, poor infrastructure, the lack of safe roads through the mountains, and a government that doesn't care about the people living in these rural farming communities, illiteracy presents a huge obstacle to the Quechua understanding God's word.

REFLECTIONS FROM ANDES TREK 2022

Mark Kaprive, CM Global's director, commented on the effectiveness of the Andes treks, saying,

> The Peru trek gives PBA students an opportunity to experience a fresh vision of the awe of creation and God's Kingdom life as they walk with their Creator and others in community on rocky and dusty trails to bring them God's word and share the Living Water of Jesus in remote villages. Where people are seeking purpose, light and something more in their heart—AWI shows up! PBA students are impacted as they impact others and see the joy when they receive Bibles—God's grand love story—in their own language for the first time.[20]

Mark has instituted a formal debrief process for students who have been sent on any mission trip by PBA. The day after returning, they are interviewed and share their impressions. They follow up with short, written reports with their thoughts and reflections. Included below are excerpts from four students who went on Andes Trek 2022.

> One thing God taught me on this trip was falling more in love with Him. In creation on the mountain tops and the valleys, you truly see His hand in the immense beauty,

---

20. Mark Kaprive, text message to author, Jan. 6, 2024. Used with permission.

there really are no words for how great God is. I want to apply my love for Him each day. I want it to be evident in each word, in my actions and in my faith, I live out each day. I hope to seek God more and more each day and to fall in love with Him more and more each day. . . . God never said this life would be easy, but He did say He'd be right by my side each step of the way. I honestly wanted to give up at one point on this trip. My body was exhausted, toes numb, feet blistered, and out of water, but I remembered that we are not only told that we can do all things through Christ who gives us strength, also we are told that He takes all our burdens while we take up His light yoke.

God showed me a bit more of what it would be like to do missions in my future. I was able to ask people more direct questions about their beliefs and share my life for Jesus with them. I am so grateful for the ways that God has grown me through this experience. I also learned that I can start now to support missionaries and missions. . . . Handing out a Bible that's just been completed and translated in someone's mother tongue for the first time has an impact on them of course—but also on you. I kept thinking of all the verse[s] that have impacted me and spoken to me and change me. Now they get to read it themselves. . . . Now families in Peru have access to the Bible in their language in their homes. Now it's God who will be revealing Himself to them through His Word.

My yes is on the table for missions. I don't really know where [God] wants me, but if it is [overseas] reaching the unreached then I am okay with that. Time with Him is irreplaceable and essential. It feeds me and I need it. . . . God used wildly unqualified and misfit people from America to bring His word to people that have never seen it before. He took me, an out of shape, ill-equipped, poor Spanish speaking loser and gave me the privilege of being the one to hand His word to people for the first time. And in that process, He showed us the value of His word and the spiritual impact it has on the people it touches. We were guided by men in the village who were ultimately ordained by God in every step of our journey. He was the one who tested the ground for us and protected us on the narrow roads, the drop-off cliffs, and the freezing nights. He was the Good Shepard for the entire trip and His role didn't change when we left the mountains. He was all of our strength, all of our provision, and all of our support and He still is. One man and his family desperately [need] His support in the future. He is the only Christian in his community, and he needs some other[-]worldly help to see change in his village.

When I think of Peru, I think of joy. There were so many highs that I experienced. There were lows too, but very little. All we did was pass out Bibles but it was so humbling because some of the villages we went to were untouched. I was giving the Word of God for the first time to somebody. He made me realize that sometimes I take the Bible for granted and go many days without even touching it. For these people they'll be able to read it for themselves, in their language. What a gift that is! . . . I also want to continue to encourage the Christian family whether it be with money or letters I write. They opened my eyes to do missions in the future with nursing and I've never thought about that until now. . . . One thing that was on my mind during the trip was that planting seeds is what makes some of the biggest impacts. We met a family one morning and learned that they are the only Christians in their village. . . . The entire team never complained. . . . It was crazy. People got sick, dizzy, tired but we all pushed through it. We were there for one reason, to plant seeds in the villages. Nothing else mattered.

SUMMARY

In this chapter I explained how both the students and I have the opportunity to fulfill PBA's mission to "extend hands" through a unique missional opportunity in the Peruvian Andes. This trip grew out of my friendship with Global Faith Mission's director, Roy Seals, and a decades'-long relationship with our host family, the Yanacs in Peru. That first trip to Venezuela in 1998 was the trip that changed everything. It opened my eyes to the need for ongoing mission work in the developing world, it offered me an opportunity to become personally involved in missions, and now I have the opportunity to share this blessing with my students.

Their debriefs tell me they caught the importance of sharing their faith:

- "I was able to ask people more direct questions about their beliefs and share my life for Jesus with them."
- "[God] took me, an out of shape, ill-equipped, poor Spanish speaking loser and gave me the privilege of being the one to hand His word to people for the first time."
- "I was giving the Word of God for the first time to somebody. . . . One thing that was on my mind during the trip was that planting seeds is what makes some of the biggest impacts. . . . We were there for one reason, to plant seeds in the villages. Nothing else mattered."

Not every professor at a Christian university will have the opportunity to lead a short-term mission trip with a group of students. Nevertheless, students need to see their professors are serious about sharing their faith. I think that it is more impactful if students can see evangelism modeled on a short-term mission trip and especially to an unreached people group in the developing world.

Jesus said, "Go into all the world and proclaim the gospel to the whole creation" (Mark 16:15). Time is short. Eternity is long. People are waiting to hear the good news. The need is for more people to be willing to go and to take God's word to them, to "extend hands."

"The harvest is plentiful, but the laborers are few. Therefore, pray earnestly to the Lord of the harvest to send out laborers into his harvest" (Luke 10:2).

CHAPTER EIGHT

Conclusion and Success Metrics

We ought, whenever we speak of God, and of His attributes, to stand in great awe.

—Robert Boyle (1627–1691)[1]

INTRODUCTION

THIS PROJECT IS THE culmination of approximately three years of research that began shortly after the COVID-19 pandemic during the fall 2020 semester when we returned to in-person classes. It includes surveys, informal interviews, and excerpts from hundreds of essays that my students have written as faith integration assignments. The project continues to evolve. While some of the practices detailed in this paper have been, of necessity, designed to speak into the lives of science students and professors, this project can serve as a helpful template for other professors teaching in different disciplines to implement a similar plan with course-specific

---

1. Blattman, "Quotes from Great Christian Scientists," para. 18. Robert Boyle is considered one of the pioneers of modern chemistry.

adjustments. I have sought to awaken an understanding of the *imago Dei* in the minds of Gen Z students through a variety of creative, gospel-centered approaches. In this final chapter, I will offer a summary of the major parts of the project, how and why they were designed specifically to impact Gen Z, and additional thoughts on measuring outcomes.

REACHING GEN Z WITH THE GOSPEL

While much of what I have described in this project is personal, it is also applicable and transferrable to any professor teaching at a Christian university. How much or how little is implemented depends somewhat on one's imagination, but more so upon one's willingness to adopt a ministry-oriented mindset and particular goals about connecting with Gen Z students.

Everything I have read about reaching Gen Z with the gospel includes practices such as being real, being kind, being patient, exhibiting mercy and justice in our character, conduct, and conversation, and offering friendship.[2] If I were to offer a template for the implementation of this project that would go a long way to fulfill those goals mentioned above, it would be to mirror the approach Jesus took with his disciples. He first got to know them. He ate with them. He spent time with them—i.e., he "did life" with them. He taught them and modeled truths for life. And he patiently mentored them. I have had some push back from professors who said they felt they would lose the respect of their students if they treated them like this, especially if they turned their school offices into hospitality zones.[3] This never seemed to bother Jesus!

Since humans do not have the luxury of omniscience, we first have to get to know our students. They have to be more than a name on an attendance record from the registrar's office. I was fortunate to come across the article "A Sisterhood of Nurses"[4]

---

2. Elliott, "Seven Ways to Reach Gen Z."
3. This was the objection of a professor who attended my seminar on hospitality.
4. See chapter 2.

CONCLUSION AND SUCCESS METRICS

early on. When I assigned this for the first time in the spring 2019 semester, it was not with the intention that students would "tell all." If a professor wishes to minister to his students effectively, he has to find a way to get to know them. It is my experience that faculty are not short on creativity, but are reluctant to become vulnerable. Spend time with students outside of class. Share a meal with them off campus or sit with them in the cafeteria, or at chapel. Our volleyball coach takes the entire team to chapel once a week and they sit together. My colleague whose office is adjacent to mine now has a tray of snacks for students in her office. And we are in the process of turning the area outside of our offices into a small student lounge. Rice University professor of chemistry Dr. James Tour invites students to his home every Sunday for dinner. Model Jesus. That is the best template.

In "Reaching Generation Z with the Gospel," Steve Sang Cheol Moon explains, "Engaging Gen Zers in conversation about Christ takes authentic relationship-building based on trust and empathy, because this generation hungers for real relationships. Gen Zers need to learn the biblical worldview by practicing it, *modeling after someone who loves it.*"[3] The whole of this project has been designed to work toward this end.

In chapter 1, I explained my vision for my students is for them to become people for whom "Jesus Christ is preeminent."[6] If I want my students living out this vision for their lives, it has to be first lived out in mine—Jesus Christ must be preeminent in my classroom, in my school office, and wherever else I might be, on or off campus.

In chapter 2, I explained the importance of knowing my students "firsthand by practicing participant observation and ethnographic interviews."[7]

In chapter 3, I demonstrated an extravagant and intentional ethos of hospitality in my school office, creating a quiet learning space that is "clean, organized, and comfortable . . . [where

---

5. Moon, "Reaching Generation Z," para. 1. Italics added.
6. Elzinga, "Christian Higher Education," 16.
7. Moon, "Reaching Generation Z," para. 17.

students] should be able to enjoy the freedom of moving around, eating and drinking, while listening . . . in an atmosphere of comfort, friendliness, and warmth adapted to their preferences."[8]

In chapters 4 and 5, I have modeled the importance of faith integration in the science classroom and laboratory, and by assigning students the same opportunities, I have let them thrive on being "situated in the middle of the learning process, as [participants] and not just remain as [observers.]"[9]

In chapter 6, I described my involvement in the School of Ministry's program to lead a CLG as an alternate chapel experience for students. This is not a lecture. They don't sit in their chairs and listen to me preach to them for an hour. It is a discussion. It creates a forum for me to "appreciate *their* questions and suggestions." They have an opportunity to share *their* insights and practice "reverse mentoring."[10]

And finally, in chapter 7, I explained how I have introduced students to an annual trip to promote Scripture to indigenous Quechua living the Andes Mountains in Peru. Through the cooperation of CM Global, the university's missions department, students don't only learn about indigenous cultures in South America, but experience them, being "in the middle of the learning process," as I mentioned above.

Gen Z's desire to do, not just observe, coupled with their FOMO (Fear of Missing Out), has created an unsettledness in their lives, helping them to "remain open to God's purposes."[11] Many have developed relationships "that transcend their physical locations,"[12] creating a desire to learn new languages and cultures. This is a characteristic that leaders can take advantage of and direct towards kingdom purposes. When members of Gen Z choose to "embody and explain the truth" in a meaningful way, and this is done with the furtherance of the gospel in mind—for example, in a

8. Moon, "Reaching Generation Z," paras. 15, 19.
9. Moon, "Reaching Generation Z," para. 15.
10. Moon, "Reaching Generation Z," para. 18. Italics added.
11. Bugnar, "Don't Miss Gen Z's Potential," para. 9.
12. Bugnar, "Don't Miss Gen Z's Potential," point 2.

foreign mission field—they can excel on a short-term mission trip or even as career missionaries.[13]

Despite Gen Z's warts, many of their distinguishing characteristics afford professors at Christian universities unparalleled opportunities to help them achieve an understanding of their identity in Christ through a comprehensive understanding of the gospel—for "the gospel changes everything."[14]

I have shared Gen Z's hunger for the truth in a myriad of ways, expressed in their own words in essays and commentaries, the excerpts of which I have shared in this project. I have had informal conversations with many, in my office and outside of class on a variety of topics not limited to Christianity and the Bible. They openly discuss their challenges, including those involving mental health. All are rooted in spiritual problems. They are looking for adult mentors in whom they can place their trust. While I am always willing to listen, my role as their professor in loco parentis gives me the authority to help them through almost whatever crisis it is they are dealing with.[15]

Not a day goes by that I don't have the opportunity to come alongside at least one student and remind them, "though [we] walk in the midst of trouble, You will revive me; You will stretch forth Your hand against the wrath of my enemies, and Your right hand will save me" (Ps 138:7).

MEASURING SUCCESS

How we measure the successes of reaching Gen Z with the gospel is a subject of ongoing research. Qualitative assessments from anecdotal observations of students' behavior—comments made to

13. Bugnar, "Don't Miss Gen Z's Potential," para. 11.

14. Almost every episode of Timothy Keller's *Gospel in Life* podcast includes what has become the ministry's signature tagline—"The gospel changes everything."

15. Except admissions of self-harm, thoughts of or attempted suicide, and sexual abuse. I am required by law to report these types of issues to the proper authorities at school.

their peers, roommates, and in online forums like "Rate My Professor"—may provide some insight whether a professor is reaching his students for Christ.

Perhaps even less meaningful are the course evaluations our university includes on its learning management system. Students are encouraged to rank fifteen "Question Texts"—e.g., Did the course cause positive feelings towards the field?—with a range of responses from "strongly disagree" to "strongly agree."

These questions may be helpful from an academic perspective, but they are unhelpful and even irrelevant to assess whether Christian values are being integrated by the professor in his course content. One question out of the fifteen comes close: "Did the course encourage Christian principles and ideas?" How course evaluations can be improved to reflect the goals of this project is one area for further research.

Measuring the Successes of CLGs

The attendance records our School of Ministry keeps for students attending CLGs is helpful, but can be misleading. Attendance is a number and chapel is a requirement. Students need chapel credits. A better metric in this regard would be consistent attendance to a specific CLG.

A qualitative assessment can be garnered from the discussions that students initiate and participate in during the actual small group meeting. Questions and conversations which follow after the meetings in informal settings—in the campus dining hall or in my office, for example—provide an additional metric for measuring the spiritual growth of students.

Baylor University's Perry L. Glanzer, professor of educational foundations, is also concerned about reaching his university's students for Christ. He commented in an email that his school's mixed-methods study revealed "our students didn't think one big mandatory chapel helped with their spiritual growth and perhaps even hindered it." This is in keeping with what I learned from the comments of several of my students who attended my CLG almost every week.[16] "The good news," Dr. Glanzer added, "is that *not one student had anything negative to say about chapel alternatives*. In fact, they spoke positively about them."[17]

In addition to this study, Dr. Glanzer has helped develop a quantitative assessment of spirituality and religious beliefs among seniors. The school asks students to indicate—Not Applicable (0), Weakened (1), No Change (2), Strengthened (3)—in what ways the following experiences have changed their religious and/or spiritual beliefs:

- Relationship with my roommate
- Involvement with campus Christian group
- Involvement with another student group
- Living on campus
- Living off campus
- Required religion courses
- Other general education courses
- Courses in my major
- Chapel
- Relationships with faculty
- Relationships with campus staff
- Relationships with friends
- Involvement with church or place of worship

A survey such as this should be an integral part of any Christian university's program of student development. Perhaps students should be required to fill out such an assessment every year beginning at the end of their freshman year so that their progress could be monitored over the next three years until graduation.[18]

16. See the student comments in chapter 6.
17. Dr. Perry Glanzer, email to author, Jan. 4, 2023. Baylor has forty-four different "small chapel experiences" that they offer to their students.
18. Dr. Glanzer explains: "At one time, we did survey first years, juniors,

My student questionnaire, administered over three semesters to 127 students, discovered that 22 percent said that "they do not have a regular time of Bible reading and prayer, and they would like guidance in this area."[19] This is a cry for help. Are we listening? I close with the words of Dr. Kenneth G. Elzinga:

> Christian higher education does not start with Christian students. . . . If prospective students who are academically qualified want to be a part of Christian higher education, they should be welcome. If the Christian faith is defensible, if the Christian faith is compelling, if the Christian faith is true, non-Christian students should be welcome to live and learn in the environment of Christian higher education and test the faith. Just as Jesus did not throw out Doubting Thomas, Christian higher education should be an environment that welcomes Doubting Thomases, as students.[20]

Our students are counting on us to lead them into all truth. Jesus said he was "the way, and the truth, and the life" (John 14:6). May we as Christian professors be committed to our students' spiritual growth in following Christ.

---

and seniors. However, especially after COVID, our response rates have been down, so we stopped surveying juniors. Survey fatigue is the main reason. That being said, we currently have more data than we can analyze."

19. See Table 1 Fall–Spring 2022–2023, Fall 2023–2024 (Three Semesters) Faith Journey Survey, 6. [X-REF]

20. Elzinga, "Christian Higher Education," 11.

Bibliography

All About History. "1918 Influenza: The Deadliest Pandemic in History." Live Science, last updated Aug. 2, 2022. https://www.livescience.com/spanish-flu.html.

Allen, Roland. *Missionary Methods: St. Paul's or Ours?* Chicago: Moody, 1956.

American Psychological Association. *Stress in AmericaTM 2020: A National Mental Health Crisis*. APA, October 2020. https://www.apa.org/news/press/releases/stress/2020/sia-mental-health-crisis.pdf.

Anderson, Courtney. *To the Golden Shore: The Life of Adoniram Judson*. Valley Forge, PA: Judson Press, 1987.

Anderson, Garwood P. "Hospitality." In *Lexham Theological Wordbook*, edited by Douglas Mangum et al. Logos ed. Bellingham, WA: Lexham, 2014.

Ansberry, Clare. "Why Middle-Aged Americans Aren't Going Back to Church." *Wall Street Journal*, Aug. 1, 2023. https://www.wsj.com/articles/church-attendance-religion-generation-x-6ee5f11d.

Augustine, Saint. *On Christian Teaching*. Translated by R. P. H. Green. Oxford World's Classics. Oxford: Oxford University Press, 2008.

Babcock, Maltbie D. "This Is My Father's World." Hymnary, 1901. https://hymnary.org/text/this_is_my_fathers_world_and_to_my.

Bannon, Lisa. "When AI Overrules the Nurses Caring for You." *Wall Street Journal*, June 15, 2023. https://www.wsj.com/articles/ai-medical-diagnosis-nurses-f881bofe.

Barna and Impact 360 Institute. *Gen Z*. Vol. 2. Barna Group, 2021.

Baumgart, Carola. *Johannes Kepler, Life and Letters*. New York: Philosophical Library, 1951.

Beaubien, Jason. "Peru Has the Highest COVID Death Rate. Here's Why." NPR, Nov. 27, 2021. Heard on *Morning Edition*. https://www.npr.org/sections/goatsandsoda/2021/11/27/1057387896/peru-has-the-worlds-highest-covid-death-rate-heres-why.

Bennett, Stephanie. *Silence, Civility, and Sanity: Hope for Humanity in a Digital Age*. Washington, DC: Lexington, 2022.

BIBLIOGRAPHY

Bergström, Lars. "Dark Matter Evidence, Particle Physics Candidates and Detection Methods." *Annalen der Physik* 524 (2012) 479–96. https://doi.org/10.1002/andp.201200116.

Berkowitz, Jacob. "On the Origins of 'We Are Stardust.'" American Institute of Physics, June 23, 2016. https://www.aip.org/news/2016/origins-we-are-stardust.

Bernstein, Elizabeth. "How to Deal with Stress in Your Life: Embrace It." *Wall Street Journal*, Aug. 28, 2021. https://www.wsj.com/articles/how-to-deal-with-stress-in-your-life-embrace-it-11630152000.

Bettenhausen, Craig. "Chemistry in Pictures: Alchemy or Intro Chem?" *Chemical and Engineering News*, Aug. 21, 2019. https://cen.acs.org/education/undergraduate-education/Chemistry-Pictures-Alchemy-intro-chem/97/web/2019/08.

Blattman, Curt. "James Joule—The Scientist Who Was Guided by God." Bible Apologetics, Jan. 14, 2021. https://bibleapologetics.org/james-joule-the-scientist-who-was-guided-by-god/.

———. "Quotes from Great Christian Scientists on God." Bible Apologetics, Oct. 17, 2021. https://bibleapologetics.org/quotes-from-great-christian-scientists-on-god/.

———. "Quotes on God and the Bible by Isaac Newton." Bible Apologetics, Aug. 17, 2021. https://bibleapologetics.org/quotes-on-god-and-the-bible-by-isaac-newton/.

Boyle, Robert. "Of the high veneration man's intellect owes to God, peculiarly for his wisdom and power." University of Michigan Library Digital Collections, 1685. https://name.umdl.umich.edu/A29013.0001.001.

Bridges, Jerry. *The Discipline of Grace*. Colorado Springs: Nav Press, 2006.

Britannica. "Ancash Earthquake of 1970." Last updated May 24, 2024. https://www.britannica.com/event/Ancash-earthquake-of-1970.

Brown, Devin. *A Life Observed*. Grand Rapids: Brazos, 2013.

Bugnar, Chip. "Don't Miss Gen Z's Missionary Potential." Gospel Coalition, Sept. 3, 2023. https://www.thegospelcoalition.org/article/gen-zs-missionary-potential/#:~:text=Gen%20Zers%20are%20attentive%20to,God's%20purposes%20in%20their%20olives.

Burge, Ryan. "There's No Crisis of Faith on Campus." *Wall Street Journal*, Feb. 24, 2022. https://www.wsj.com/articles/theres-no-crisis-of-faith-on-campus-11645714717.

Byma, Elizabeth. "Hospitality and Nursing." *Christian Scholar's Review*, Dec. 8, 2021. https://christianscholars.com/guest-post-hospitality-nursing/.

Chapell, Bryan. *Christ-Centered Preaching: Redeeming the Expository Sermon*. Grand Rapids: Baker, 1994.

———. "The Components and Process of Exposition." Lecture 9 from Christ-Centered Preaching, doctoral course at Knox Theological Seminary, transcribed by Gregory J. Rummo.

BIBLIOGRAPHY

———. "Evangelistic Preaching in a Post-Modern Era for the Churched." Lecture 33 from Christ-Centered Preaching, doctoral course at Knox Theological Seminary, transcribed by Gregory J. Rummo.

———. "Exploring New Listeners in a Post-Modern Era." Lecture 32 from Christ-Centered Preaching, doctoral course at Knox Theological Seminary, transcribed by Gregory J. Rummo.

———. *Unlimited Grace: The Heart Chemistry That Frees from Sin and Fuels the Christian Life.* Wheaton, IL: Crossway, 2016.

Christianity.com. "What Does 'Imago Dei' Mean? The Image of God in the Bible." Oct. 21, 2022. https://www.christianity.com/wiki/bible/image-of-god-meaning-imago-dei-in-the-bible.html.

Coffman, Elesha. "Where Did Small Groups Start?" *Christianity Today*, Aug. 8, 2008. https://www.christianitytoday.com/2008/08/where-did-small-groups-start/.

Collins, Phil. "Another Day in Paradise." Songfacts. https://www.songfacts.com/facts/phil-collins/another-day-in-paradise.

Corbett, Steve, and Brian Fikkert. *When Helping Hurts: How to Alleviate Poverty Without Hurting the Poor . . . and Yourself.* Chicago: Moody, 2014.

Corey, Benjamin L. "Christian Ghosting: The Destructive Christian Practice We Don't Talk About." https://www.benjaminlcorey.com/christian-ghosting-destructive-christian-practice-dont-talk/.

C. S. Lewis Institute. "Reflections: Longing for Home." Jan. 1, 2010. https://www.cslewisinstitute.org/resources/reflections-january-2010/.

Cuncic, Arlin. "Why Gen Z Is More Open to Talking About Their Mental Health." Very Well Mind, Mar. 25, 2021. https://www.verywellmind.com/why-gen-z-is-more-open-to-talking-about-their-mental-health-5104730.

Delaware Bible Church. "History of the Quechua Bible Translation." Narrated by Rachel Yanac. Facebook. https://www.facebook.com/DelawareBible/videos/2998091833595443/.

Dembski, William, et al., eds. *The Comprehensive Guide to Science and Faith.* Eugene, OR: Harvest House, 2021.

DeSteno, David. "Is Religion Good for Your Health?" *Wall Street Journal*, June 8, 2023. https://www.wsj.com/articles/is-religion-good-for-your-health-921814a7.

Dockery, David S., and David P. Gushee. *The Future of Christian Higher Education.* Nashville: B&H, 1999.

Dreher, Rod. *The Benedict Option: A Strategy for Christians in a Post-Christian Nation.* New York: Sentinel, 2017.

Drew, Christopher. "Why Science Majors Change Their Minds (It's Just So Darn Hard)." *New York Times*, Nov. 4, 2011.

Duncan, Maryann. "The Meaning Behind the Song: Kiss from a Rose by Seal." BeatCrave, Apr. 23, 2024. https://beatcrave.com/the-meaning-behind-the-song-kiss-from-a-rose-by-seal/.

BIBLIOGRAPHY

Eglinton, James. "Tim Keller and American Neo-Calvinism." Gospel Coalition (podcast), Nov. 24, 2023. https://www.thegospelcoalition.org/podcasts/tgc-podcast/tim-keller-neo-calvinism/.

Elliott, Bryn S. "Seven Ways for Churches to Reach Gen Z." *Tithe.ly*, May 25, 2023. https://get.tithe.ly/blog/7-ways-for-churches-to-reach-gen-z.

Elliot, Elisabeth. *Through Gates of Splendor*. Lincoln: Tyndale, 2005.

Elzinga, Kenneth G. "Christian Higher Education vs. Christians in Higher Education." In *A Higher Education: Baylor and the Vocation of a Christian University*, edited by Elizabeth Davis. Waco: Baylor University Press, 2012.

Estep, James R., Jr., et al. *A Theology for Christian Education*. Nashville: B&H Academic, 2008.

Feed. "What We Know About Gen Z." 2020. https://feed.bible/research/.

Feintzeig, Rachel. "Stressed Nurses Wonder: How to Quit a Job When It's Your Calling?" *Wall Street Journal*, Jan. 10, 2022. https://www.wsj.com/articles/when-youre-burned-out-at-your-job-but-its-also-your-calling-11641790863.

Foley, Eric. "'Prevenient Grace': The Theological Term for 'Hospitality.'" *Do the Word*, Feb. 29, 2012. https://dotheword.org/2012/02/29/prevenient-grace-the-theological-term-for-hospitality/.

Frame, John M. *The Doctrine of the Christian Life: A Theology of Lordship*. Phillipsburg, NJ: P&R, 2008.

Francis, Andrew. *Hospitality and Community After Christendom*. Authentic Media, 2014. ProQuest Ebook Central.

Frankel, Todd. C. "The Cobalt Pipeline." *Washington Post*, Sept. 30, 2016. https://www.washingtonpost.com/graphics/business/batteries/congo-cobalt-mining-for-lithium-ion-battery/?tid=a_inl.

Fuller, Steven. "Foreword." In *Theistic Evolution: A Scientific, Philosophical, and Theological Critique*, edited by J. P. Moreland et al., 12–15. Wheaton, IL: Crossway, 2017.

Glanzer, Perry. *Christian Higher Education: An Empirical Guide*. Abilene: Abilene Christian University Press, 2023.

Goldsworthy, Graeme. *According to Plan: The Unfolding Revelation of God in the Bible*. Nottingham, UK: Inter-Varsity Press, 1991.

Guillen, Michael. *Amazing Truths: How Science and the Bible Agree*. Grand Rapids: Zondervan, 2016.

———. "The Bible and Science: The Ultimate Power Couple." Fox News, Feb. 9, 2016. https://www.foxnews.com/opinion/the-bible-and-science-the-ultimate-power-couple.

Gushee, David. "Making Room: Recovering Hospitality as a Christian Tradition." *Christian Ethics Today*, Dec. 27, 2010. https://christianethicstoday.com/wp/making-room-recovering-hospitality-as-a-christian-tradition/.

Haines, David. "Does Science Conflict with Biblical Faith?" *The Comprehensive Guide to Science and Faith*, edited by William A. Dembski et al., 67–81. Eugene, OR: Harvest House, 2021.

BIBLIOGRAPHY

Harris, James T. "A Walk in the Canyon." Inside Higher Ed, July 14, 2023. https://www.insidehighered.com/opinion/career-advice/2023/07/14/president-shares-benefits-walks-students-opinion.

Harris, Murray J. *Slave of Christ: A New Testament Metaphor for Total Devotion to Christ*. Downers Grove, IL: Inter Varsity, 1999.

Howes, Laura. "Scenes from Where Chemists Work." *Chemical & Engineering News* 101 (2023). https://cen.acs.org/people/Scenes-from-where-chemists-work/101/i32.

ISCAST. "Study Suggests That Gen Z Have a More Balanced Perspective Towards the Relationship Between Science and Religion." Jan, 17, 2023. https://iscast.org/news/study-suggests-a-more-balanced-perspective-towards-the-relationship-between-science-and-religion-in-younger-generations/.

Jaeger, Lydia. "Science and Theology as Gifts to the Church: How Creation Allows Scientists and Theologians to Work Together." *Perspectives on Science and Christian Faith* 74 (2022) 3–18.

Janin, Alex. "Starting School Before 8 a.m. Can Be Harmful to Teens, Sleep Scientists Say." *Wall Street Journal*, Sept. 27, 2022. https://www.wsj.com/articles/high-schools-are-starting-too-early-sleep-scientists-say-11664248551.

Jenkins, Ryan. "3 Things Making Gen Z the Loneliest Generation." *Psychology Today*, Aug. 16, 2022. https://www.psychologytoday.com/us/blog/the-case-connection/202208/3-things-making-gen-z-the-loneliest-generation.

Jewish Virtual Library. "Hospitality." https://www.jewishvirtuallibrary.org/hospitality.

Keller, Timothy. *Center Church: Doing Balanced, Gospel-Centered Ministry in Your City*. Grand Rapids: Zondervan, 2012.

———. *Encounters with Jesus: Unexpected Answers to Life's Biggest Questions*. New York: Penguin Books, 2016.

———. *The Freedom of Self-Forgetfulness: The Path to True Christian Joy*. New York: 10Publishing, 2012.

———. "Preaching in a Secular Culture." Gospel in Life, Jan. 4, 2010. https://gospelinlife.com/manual-paper/preaching-in-a-secular-culture/.

———. *Prodigal God: Recovering the Heart of the Christian Faith*. New York: Penguin Books, 2011.

Klein, Camilla. "The Ultimate Guide to Christian Hospitality: What the Bible Says." Christian Educators Academy, Sept. 12, 2024. https://christianeducatorsacademy.com/the-ultimate-guide-to-christian-hospitality-what-the-bible-says/.

Komisar, Erica. "Legal Weed Feeds the Teen Mental-Health Crisis." *Wall Street Journal*, Mar. 1, 2023. https://www.wsj.com/articles/legal-weed-feeds-the-teen-mental-health-crisis-psychosis-anxiety-depression-depersonalization-jama-marijuana-e2d81752.

Krish, John and Peter Sykes, dirs. *The Jesus Film*. 1979. https://www.jesusfilm.org/watch/jesus.html/english.html.

BIBLIOGRAPHY

Lagnado, Lucette. "A Sisterhood of Nurses." *Wall Street Journal*, Aug. 11, 2018. https://www.wsj.com/articles/a-sisterhood-of-nurses-1533992461.

Lamont, Ann. "Great Creation Scientists: James Clerk Maxwell." *Creation* 15 (1993) 45–47. https://creation.com/great-creation-scientists-james-clerk-maxwell.

———. "Louis Pasteur (1822–1895): Outstanding Scientist and Opponent of Evolution." *Creation* 14 (1991) 16–19. https://creation.com/louis-pasteur.

Lewis, C. S. *God in the Dock*. Edited by Walter Hooper. Grand Rapids: Eerdmans, 1970.

———. *Mere Christianity*. New York: Harper Collins, 1980.

———. *The Weight of Glory*. New York: Macmillan, 1966.

Lints, Richard. *The Fabric of Theology: A Prolegomenon to Evangelical Theology*. Grand Rapids: Eerdmans, 1993.

Litfin, Duane. *Conceiving the Christian College*. Grand Rapids: Eerdmans, 2004.

Livgren, Kerry. "Dust in the Wind." Songfacts, 1977. https://www.songfacts.com/facts/kansas/dust-in-the-wind.

Mark, Gloria. "How to Restore Our Dwindling Attention Span." *Wall Street Journal*, Jan. 6, 2023. https://www.wsj.com/articles/how-to-restore-our-attention-spans-11673031247.

Marty, Martin E. "Freud and Other 'God-Killers' Are Here to Stay." University of Chicago Divinity School, Oct. 2, 2017. https://divinity.uchicago.edu/sightings/articles/freud-and-other-god-killers-are-here-stay#:~:text=share%20email%20share-,Darwin-Marx-Nietzsche-Freud—dubbable%2C%20and%20sometimes,God"%20for%20some%20future%20column.

Matthews-King, Alex. "Generation Z Teenagers Have More Mental Health Problems Despite Drops in Smoking, Drugs and Antisocial Behavior." *Independent*, Feb. 7, 2019. https://www.the-independent.com/news/health/teenage-depression-mental-health-drugs-antisocial-behaviour-generation-z-a8800291.html.

McNally, Richard J. "'The Good Life' Review: The Habit of Happiness." *Wall Street Journal*, Jan. 11, 2023. https://www.wsj.com/articles/the-good-life-review-the-habit-of-happiness-11673478213.

Meyer, Stephen C. *The Return of the God Hypothesis: Three Scientific Discoveries That Reveal the Mind Behind the Universe*. New York: Harper One, 2021.

Miller, Paul. *A Praying Life: Connecting with God in a Distracting World*. Colorado Springs: NavPress, 2017.

Mitchell, Joni. "Woodstock." AZLyrics, 1970. https://www.azlyrics.com/lyrics/jonimitchell/woodstock.html.

Moo, Douglas J. *The Letter to the Romans*. New International Commentary on the New Testament. Grand Rapids: Eerdmans, 2018.

Moon, Steve Sang-Cheol. "Reaching Generation Z with the Gospel." *Lausanne Global Analysis* 10 (2021). https://lausanne.org/global-analysis/reaching-generation-z-with-the-gospel.

BIBLIOGRAPHY

Morris, Betsy. "How Old Do You Feel? The Answer Can Reveal a Lot About Your Health, Scientists Say." *Wall Street Journal*, Dec. 5, 2022. https://www.wsj.com/articles/can-feeling-younger-improve-health-subjective-age-11670009137.

Murphy, Kate. "The Covid Fear Isn't Going Anywhere for a While." *Wall Street Journal*, Aug. 15, 2021. https://www.wsj.com/articles/anxiety-covid-delta-variant-11628796175.

Neill, Stephen. *A History of Christian Missions*. New York: Penguin Books, 1991.

Nouwen, Henri J. M. *Reaching Out: The Three Movements of the Spiritual Life*. New York: Doubleday, 1975.

Office of the Historian. "The Cuban Missile Crisis, October 1962." https://history.state.gov/milestones/1961-1968/cuban-missile-crisis.

Packer, J. I. *In My Place Condemned He Stood: Celebrating the Glory of the Atonement*. Wheaton, IL: Crossway, 2007.

Palm Beach Atlantic University. "Campus Ministries and CMGlobal." https://www.pba.edu/campus-life/christian-community/student-missions/.

———. "Chapel." https://www.pba.edu/campus-life/christian-community/chapel/index.html.

———. "Guiding Principles." https://www.pba.edu/campus-life/christian-community/guiding-principles.html.

———. "Values and Guiding Principles." https://www.pba.edu/campus-life/christian-community/values/.

———. "Workship." https://www.pba.edu/campus-life/christian-community/workship/.

Petersen, Andrea. "A Rise in Suicides by Young Children Leaves Families Searching for Answers." *Wall Street Journal*, June 5, 2022. https://www.wsj.com/articles/a-rise-in-suicides-by-young-children-leaves-families-searching-for-answers-11654389545.

Phillips, Lindsey. "The Emotional and Social Health Needs of Gen Z." *Counseling Today*, Jan. 10, 2022. https://www.counseling.org/publications/counseling-today-magazine/article-archive/article/legacy/the-emotional-and-social-health-needs-of-gen-z#.

Piper, John. *Don't Waste Your Life*. Wheaton, IL: Crossway, 2003.

Pitts, Guy. "The Meaning Behind the Song: Disappear by Hoobastank." BeatCrave, May 25, 2024. https://beatcrave.com/the-meaning-behind-the-song-disappear-by-hoobastank/.

Pohl, Christine. *Making Room: Hospitality as a Christian Tradition*. Grand Rapids: Eerdmans, 1999.

Richardson, Don. *Eternity in Their Hearts*. Minneapolis: Baker, 1981.

Richter, Kyle, and Patrick Miller. "How to Feed Gen Z's Hunger for Jesus." Gospel Coalition, Nov. 4, 2023. https://www.thegospelcoalition.org/article/gen-zs-hunger/.

Rolston, Holmes, III. *Science and Religion: A Critical Survey*. Philadelphia: Temple University Press, 1987.

Rummo, Gregory J. "10 Suggestions for Incoming College STEM Freshmen." *Orlando Sentinel*, July 30, 2021. https://www.orlandosentinel.com/2021/07/30/10-suggestions-for-incoming-college-stem-freshmen-commentary/.

———. "Are We Living in a Christ-Animating Simulation?" *Christian Scholar's Review*, Sept. 12, 2022. https://christianscholars.com/are-we-living-in-a-christ-animating-simulation%ef%bf%bc%ef%bf%bc/.

———. "C. S. Lewis on Christian Apologetics: Needed Now More than Ever in Christian Higher Education." Minding the Campus, June 17, 2023. https://www.mindingthecampus.org/2023/06/17/c-s-lewis-on-christian-apologetics-needed-now-more-than-ever-in-christian-higher-education/.

———. "Educating the Whole Person." In *Good News Christian College Guide 2023*, 32. https://digital.goodnewsfl.org/2023/ccg/12/.

———. "Faith in the Invisible and the Nature of Reality." *Christian Scholar's Review*, Mar. 1, 2022. https://christianscholars.com/guest-post-faith-in-the-invisible-and-the-nature-of-reality/.

———. "Get a Vision. Get Off Your Cellphone. Get to Work." Minding the Campus, Mar. 11, 2023. https://www.mindingthecampus.org/2023/03/11/get-a-vision-get-off-your-cellphone-get-to-work/.

———. "Latest Discoveries in the Field of Structural Biology Point to Intelligent Design." *Christian Scholar's Review*, Nov. 19, 2021. https://christianscholars.com/guest-post-latest-discoveries-in-the-field-of-structural-biology-point-to-intelligent-design/.

———. "Listen to Their Stories Like They're Your Children." *Christian Scholar's Review*, June 9, 2023. https://christianscholars.com/listen-to-their-stories-like-theyre-your-children/.

———. "A Multi-Generational Perspective on the Covid-19 Pandemic." *Christian Scholar's Review*, Feb. 10, 2022. https://christianscholars.com/a-multi-generational-perspective-on-the-covid-19-pandemic/.

———. "Teaching Science Students to Think Critically About EVs and to Peek Behind the Curtain." *Christian Scholar's Review*, Apr. 29, 2022. https://christianscholars.com/teaching-science-students-to-think-critically-about-evs-and-to-peek-behind-the-curtain/.

———. "Ten Commandments for First-Year Chemistry." Minding the Campus, Aug. 18, 2023. https://www.mindingthecampus.org/2023/08/18/ten-commandments-for-first-year-chemistry/.

———. "They're Dying to Tell You Their Stories." Minding the Campus, June 3, 2023. https://www.mindingthecampus.org/2023/06/03/theyre-dying-to-tell-you-their-stories/.

———. *The View from the Grass Roots*. Salt Lake City: Millennial Mind, 2002.

———. *The View from the Grass Roots—Another Look*. Enumclaw, WA: Pleasant Word, 2010.

———. "What Nursing Students Can Teach Us About Life." *Christian Scholar's Review*, Apr. 1, 2022. https://christianscholars.com/what-nursing-students-can-teach-us-about-life/.

BIBLIOGRAPHY

Rutherford, Ernest, and John A. Ratcliffe. "Forty Years of Physics." In *Background to Modern Science*, edited by Joseph Needham and Walter Pagel, 49–76. Cambridge: Cambridge University Press, 1938.

Sanders, Oswald J. *Spiritual Leadership: Principles of Excellence for Every Believer*. Chicago: Moody Bible Institute Press, 2017.

Scroggins, Jimmy. "3 Circles." North American Mission Board. https://www.namb.net/resource/3-circles-sample-presentation/.

Shah, Saeed. "As Hunger Spreads in Afghanistan, Hospitals Fill with Premature, Dying Babies." *Wall Street Journal*, Jan. 28, 2022. https://www.wsj.com/articles/as-hunger-spreads-in-afghanistan-hospitals-fill-with-premature-dying-babies-11643365807.

Shermer, Michael. "The Meaning of Life in a Formula." *Scientific American Magazine* 313 (2015) 83. doi:10.1038/scientificamerican0815-83.

Simango, Daniel. "The Imago Dei (Gen 1:26–27): A History of Interpretation from Philo to the Present." *Studia Historiae Ecclesiasticae* 42 (2016) 172–90. https://doi.org/10.25159/2412-4265/1065.

Smith, James K. A. *Desiring the Kingdom: Worship, Worldview, and Cultural Formation*. Grand Rapids: Baker Academic, 2009.

Sparks, Sarah D. "Why Teacher-Student Relationships Matter." Education Week, Mar. 12, 2019. https://www.edweek.org/teaching-learning/why-teacher-student-relationships-matter/2019/03.

Sproul, R. C. "What Does 'Simul Justus et Peccator,' Mean?" Ligonier Updates, Oct. 17, 2019. https://www.ligonier.org/posts/simul-justus-et-peccator.

Starkey, Sara Barratt. "Gen Z's Identity Crisis." Summit Ministries, June 14, 2023. https://www.summit.org/resources/articles/gen-zs-identity-crisis/.

Stoltzfus, Tony. *Christian Life Coaching Handbook: Calling and Destiny Discovery Tools for Christian Life Coaching*. Virginia Beach: Coach22, 2009.

Taitz, Jenny. "Honest Communication in the Age of Ghosting." *Wall Street Journal*, Aug. 27, 2021. https://www.wsj.com/articles/honest-communication-in-the-age-of-ghosting-11630070801.

Taylor, Frederick Howard, and Geraldine Taylor. *Hudson Taylor's Spiritual Secret*. Chicago: Moody, 2009.

Thompson, Abigail. "Gen Z Needs a Place at Your Kitchen Table." Gospel Coalition, Sept. 1, 2023. https://www.thegospelcoalition.org/article/gen-z-table/.

Tucker, Ruth A. *From Jerusalem to Irian Jaya: A Biographical History of Christian Missions*. Grand Rapids: Zondervan, 2004.

Ucha, Terhemba. "The Impact of Visual Content: Captivating Your Audience's Attention." AdsTargets, Aug. 1, 2023. https://adstargets.com/blog/the-impact-of-visual-content-captivating-your-audiences-attention/.

University of Queensland. "One in Five Adolescents Have Suicidal Thoughts or Anxiety." June 22, 2020. https://www.uq.edu.au/news/article/2020/06/one-five-adolescents-have-suicidal-thoughts-or-anxiety.

Varadarajan, Tunku. "Jonathan Haidt on the 'National Crisis' of Gen Z." *Wall Street Journal*, Dec. 31, 2022. https://www.wsj.com/articles/the-national-crisis-of-generation-z-jonathan-haidt-social-media-performance-anxiety-fragility-gap-childhood-11672401345.

Waltke, Bruce. *An Old Testament Theology: An Exegetical, Canonical, and Thematic Approach*. Grand Rapids: Zondervan Academic, 2007.

West, John G., ed. *The Magician's Twin: C. S. Lewis on Science, Scientism, and Society*. Seattle: Discovery Institute, 2012.

Willis, Dustin, and Brandon Clements. *The Simplest Way to Change the World: Biblical Hospitality as a Way of Life*. Chicago: Moody, 2017.

Wingren, Gustaf. *Luther on Vocation*. Translated by Carl C. Rasmussen. 1957. Repr., Eugene, OR: Wipf & Stock, 2004.

Wright, N. T. *Simply Christian: Why Christianity Makes Sense*. New York: HarperOne, 2006.

Zylstra, Sarah Eekhoff. "How John Piper's Seashells Swept over a Generation." Gospel Coalition, Mar. 20, 2017. https://www.thegospelcoalition.org/article/how-john-pipers-seashells-swept-over-a-generation/.

Index

Advocacy (for the helpless), 84–87
Afghanistan, withdrawal from, 66–67
Anxiety, 3, 44, 45, 59, 63, 68, 74
Asociación Alli Willaqui, 104, 108, 114–15
Assignments
   1970's soft rock songs, 70–72
   faith integration essay, 22–32, 54–55
   reading, 24–25, 66–70
   social media posts, 72–74, 73
Atomic theory, 79–84
Attentiveness, 44–45
Augustine, xi, 49, 55
AWI. *see* Asociación Alli Willaqui

Balance (in life), 44
Beginning a Praying Life (Miller), 91, 92, **99**
Beyond Boundaries (Keller), 99, 102
Bible
   distribution, 114
   science and the, 48, 51
   translation into Quechua (Huaylas), 105
Biblical hospitality, 34–36
Bohr, Niels, 81

Campus Ministry Global, 112, 114, 122
Center Church (Keller), 14, 18, 19, 21, 74n56
Chaos, 54
Chapel Life Groups (CLGs), 88–89, 124
   attendance, 92, **100**
   author's experience leading a, 90–93
   material used in "Keller's Kids," 9
   students responses to, 100–102
Chapell, Bryan, 23, 33n2, 83, 88
Chemical reactions, 78
Chemistry courses
   classroom, 47–75
   integrated with science, 52–57
   laboratory, 76–87
   student demographics of, 52–53
Christ-Centered Preaching (Chapell), 33n2, 83
Christian university, characteristics of, 12, 15, 16–18
CLGs. *see* Chapel Life Groups
Community, 42–43
Consumerism, 85–86
Course evaluations, 124
COVID-19 pandemic, 3, 58, 68–69
Creation, 49, 56–57

INDEX

Credentials, 16–17

Depression, xiii, 3, 44, 45, 60, 63, 74

Eglinton, James, 18–19
Elzinga, Kenneth G., 14, 16–18, 21, 126
Encounters with Jesus (Keller), 102
Evangelism, 103–8, 110
   see also Mission trips

Faculty, gender and ethnicity, 8–9
Faith
   and career, 22
   classical scientists and, 48–50
   compatible with science, 87
   crisis of, 65–66
   integration into chemistry laboratory, 76–87
   integrated with science, 48–50
   integration into chemistry classroom, 47–75
Faith integration essays
   in chemistry classroom, 47–75
   in chemistry laboratory, 76–87
   pre-nursing students, 57–61, **58**, 74
   students' responses, 54–57, 74
Freedom of Self-Forgetfulness, The (Keller), 94–95, **99**, 101

Gen Z, xiii, 3, 22–23
   acceptance of faith and science, 50
   aging and, 69–70
   characteristics of, 122–23
   ghosting and, 63–64
   Gospel and, 120
   hospitality and, 36–38
   identity crisis, 93–94
   mental health of, 62–63
   modeling Christ, 121
   need for relationships, 121
   at Palm Beach Atlantic University, 3–4
   religious affiliation, 3
   stress from COVID pandemic, 60–61
   see also Students
Ghosting, 63–64
Glanzer, Perry L., 124–25
Global Faith Mission, 109, 117
God
   creation and, 39–40, 51
   as lab partner, 77–78
   looking for, 53
   presence of, 52
   scientists, belief in, 48–50, 77–78
   student testimonials, belief in, 25–31, 59–60, 61–62, 64, 65, 68–70, 115–17
   tragedy and, 29–30
"God awareness," 50–52
   see also imago Dei (Image of God)
Guillen, Michael, 56, 73

Happiness, 28, 67–68
Heat (joule), 84
Help, concept of, 71
Home, concept of, 96–97
Hospitality
   author's experience, 33–34
   biblical hospitality, 34–36
   Gen Z and, 36–38
   practical suggestions for faculty, 39–45
Huaylas, dialect of Quechua, 105, 107n12
Hydrogen model, 81, 82

Image of God. *see imago Dei*
imago Dei (Image of God), 10, 12, 20, 48, 50–51, 95, 97
Inspiration, 30–31

INDEX

Interviews, informal, 8, 11, 119, 123, 124

Jesus
  hospitality, 37
  as mentor, 17
  parables as visuals, 76
  as teaching model for students, 120–21
Jesus Film, 107, 113, 114
Joule, James, 84

Kaprive, Mark, 91, 112, 115
Keller, Timothy
  Beyond Boundaries, **99**, 102
  Center Church, 14, 18, 19, 21, 74n56
  Encounters with Jesus, 102
  Freedom of Self-Forgetfulness, The, 94–95, **99**
  Prodigal God, 95–98, **99**
  . see also "Keller's Kids"
"Keller's Kids," 88–102
Kepler, Johannes, 49

Laboratory techniques, 84, 87
Lewis, C.S., 20, 52, 82–83, 97–98
Lints, Richard, 19

Matter, 56–57
Maxwell, James Clerk, 78
McNally, Richard J., 58, 67
Mental health, 25, 44–45, 62, 63, 123
Mentoring, 11, 14, 17, 18, 37, 45, 122
Miller, Paul, 91, 92, **99**
Mining, lithium-cobalt, 85–86
Mission trips
  addressing illiteracy, 115
  Bible distribution, 114
  evangelization, 115
  medical, 114
  planning of, 110–15
  short-term, 108–10
  students' responses, 115–17, 118

Music (1970's soft rock songs), 51, 70–72, **72**

New Testament, 34, 36, 105, 107
Newton, Isaac, 48, 77
Nursing, faith integration, 57–61
Nursing students. *see* Pre-nursing students

Old Testament, 35, 36, 71, 105
Orderliness, 39–40, 54
Original sin (*peccatum originis*), 49–50

Palm Beach Atlantic University
  chapel attendance, 99
  culture, 10–13, 18n13
  "enlightening minds" (motto), 10, 47, 74
  "enriching souls" (motto), 10, 47
  "extending hands" (motto), 10, 102, 104
  faculty, 8–9
  faculty demographics, 8–9, **9**
  faith-based classes, 28
  mission scholarships, 111
  missions to Peru, 104, 111–15
  motto, 10
  School of Ministry, 88–89, 91, 122
  student-professor relationship, 26
Pasteur, Louis, 77–78
Paul (apostle), 17n9, 30, 35, 55, 83, 90, 110
PBA. *see* Palm Beach Atlantic University
Peruvian missions, 104, 106–8, 110–15
Physical change (vs chemical reactions), 78
Planck, Max, 48
Prayer, 40, 93, 101

INDEX

Praying Life, A (Miller), **99**
Pre-nursing students
    aging and, 69–70
    chemistry classes, 52, 53
    COVID fears, 68–69
    faith integration essay, 57–58
    personal experiences, 25–30
    reading assignment, 24–25, 66–70
    stress and, 58–61
Prodigal God (Keller), 95–98, 99

Quechua, 104–8, 113–15, 122

Religious affiliation, students, 3
Rummo, Gregory J.
    faith integration essay assignment, 22–32
    family history, 4–5
    leading a Chapel Life Group, 90–93
    missionary work in Peru, 106–8
    modeling Jesus as teaching model, 120–21
    planning for mission trips, 110–15
    summary of teaching methods, 119–26
    theological vision, 20, 22
Rutherford, Ernest, 80

School of Ministry, 88–89, 91, 122
Schrödinger, Erwin, 81–82
Scientists, their faith, 48–50
Seals, Roy, 106, 109, 110n16, 117
Self-Forgetfulness, 94–95
Serving others, 28
Short-term mission trips, 108–10
Small groups (worship meetings), 89–90
Social media, 63, 70–74
Social responsibility, in the chemistry laboratory, 84–87
Songs (1970's soft-rock), 72

Stability (structure in life), 42
Stress, xiii, 58–61, 68–69
Students
    aging and, 69–70
    community and, 42–43
    community service program, 12
    COVID-19 pandemic, 68–69
    crisis of faith, 65–66
    difficult upbringing, 28–29
    faith and, 65
    faith journey survey, 6
    family tragedy, 29–30
    ghosting and, 63–64
    habit of happiness, 67–68
    hospitality for, 39–45
    importance of sharing faith, 116–18
    informal interviews, 8, 11, 119, 123, 124
    mental health, 25, 44–45, 62, 63, 123
    mission trips, 111–15
    at Palm Beach Atlantic University, 2–7
    personal essay themes from, 26–31, **26**
    prayer, 40
    pre-nursing, 24–25, 57–61, 66
    reaction to Afghanistan withdrawal, 66–67
    religious affiliation, 3
    responses for faith integration essay, 55–57
    responses to Chapel Life Groups, 100–102
    responses to missionary work, 115–17, 118
    spiritual assessment of, 125–26
    stability (structure in life), 42
    stress, xiii, 58–61, 68–69
    suicide, xiii, 26, 44–45, 61–63
    sustenance (food), 43–44

testimonials, belief in God, 25–31, 59–60, 61–62, 64, 65, 68–70, 115–17
trauma, 26
work and, 41
see also Gen Z; pre-nursing students
Suicide, xiii, 26, 44–45, 61–63
Survey, student denomination and faith journey, 6–7
Sustenance (food), 43

Teaching, 16
    approaches to, 119–23
    vulnerability, 121
Teaching methods
    annual trips, 122
    ethnographic interviews, 119
    first person narratives, 119
    music (1970's soft rock), 70–72
    social media, 72–74

surveys and informal interviews, 119
Theological vision, 14–20
Theological vision, author's, 20, 22
Thomson, Joseph John, 80
Tragedy, 29–30
Trauma, 26

Universe, 54–57

Venezuela, 106
Visuals, 76–78

Wordship, vin1, 10, 12
Workship, vin1, 10, 12
Worship, vin1, 10, 11
Wycliffe Bible Translators, 104, 105

X (formerly Twitter), 72–74, **73**

Yanac, Adelid, 104n5, 107–8, 118

www.ingramcontent.com/pod-product-compliance
Lightning Source LLC
Chambersburg PA
CBHW070907160426
43193CB00011B/1394